TORTILLAS
TO THE RESCUE COOKBOOK

D0746095

TORTILLAS
TO THE RESCUE COOKBOOK

Scrumptious Snacks, Mouth-Watering Meals and
Delicious Desserts—All Made with the Amazing
Tortilla

Jessica Harlan

 Ulysses Press

Published by:
ULYSSES PRESS
P.O. Box 3440
Berkeley, CA 94703
www.ulyssespress.com

ISBN: 978-1-61243-100-0
Library of Congress Catalog Number 2012940431

Printed in the United States by Bang Printing

10 9 8 7 6 5 4 3 2 1

Acquisitions editor: Keith Riegert
Managing editor: Claire Chun
Editor: Lauren Harrison
Proofreader: Elyce Berrigan-Dunlop
Production: Judith Metzener
Design: what!design @ whatweb.com
Front cover photos: tortillas © travellinglight/istockphoto.com, ham sandwich © svariophoto/istockphoto.com, burrito © Lauri Patterson/istockphoto.com
Back cover photos: tortilla lime bar © Jessica Harlan, shrimp tacos © TheCrimsonMonkey/istockphoto.com

Distributed by Publishers Group West

For Chip, Sadie, and Gillian, who make it all worthwhile.
And for my mom, who fed me my first tortillas.

TABLE OF CONTENTS

ACKNOWLEDGMENTS

As I was writing this book, I came to realize how many memories and warm associations came to mind of wonderful meals I've enjoyed as the child of a New Mexican mother. Thanks, Mom, for giving me such a rich culinary background.

I am also appreciative of my friends and extended family who have helped me along the way, tasting recipes, offering suggestions, watching my children when I needed a few hours to work, and offering encouragement when I felt overwhelmed. My husband, Chip, and daughters, Sadie and Gillian, were so supportive, appreciative of even yet another tortilla recipe for dinner, and understanding when work kept me from family time. I couldn't have done it without you!

I feel so grateful to have had the opportunity to write a third cookbook for Ulysses Press, and am truly indebted to my editor Lauren, who's taught me so much about recipe writing, as well as to the rest of the staff, particularly Keith, Kourtney, Alice, and Bryce.

And finally, I've come to truly appreciate and value my readers and the food community for their support and interest in the books I've written. I am especially grateful to the bloggers who have taken the time to read my book, try out the recipes, photograph them so beautifully, and write such nice words about them. Thank you.

INTRODUCTION

When I was growing up, my New Mexico–born mother kept a bag of tortillas in the fridge like other moms kept theirs stocked with bread. Friday nights were enchiladas for my parents and burritos for my brother and me; we thought the enchilada sauce that she made from her precious stash of red chiles (replenished every time we visited my grandma in Santa Fe) was too spicy. Weekend mornings were huevos rancheros, and sometimes we'd snack on flour tortillas slathered with butter and sprinkled with cinnamon and sugar. And when we went out to dinner at our favorite neighborhood Mexican restaurant, I loved ripping off pieces of the warm flour tortillas from a seemingly bottomless Styrofoam tortilla warmer, and using the pieces to scoop up dollops of guacamole.

When I was out on my own for the first time, I quickly discovered the versatility of tortillas for myself. They didn't seem to get stale, they were inexpensive, and there was little I couldn't wrap up in the soft, floury rounds. I'd use them for everything from traditional burritos to ad hoc hot dog buns.

That was the impetus for this book. With a couple packages of flour or corn tortillas in your fridge, you'll always have a good foundation for a delicious meal, from breakfast and dinner to dessert and late-night snacks. You can even use tortillas in unexpected ways: to thicken soups, to bulk up casseroles, and even to make a crust for quiches or pies.

If, like me, you can never get your fill of tortillas, or if you're simply looking for a convenient, inexpensive shortcut ingredient to make easy, fun meals, hopefully this book will help you find a wealth of ways to use tortillas in both traditional and innovative manners.

Tortillas: A Brief Background

Tortillas are one of the simplest forms of bread, not much more than a mixture of wheat or corn flour, fat, and water, pressed flat and cooked on a hot surface. The word means "little cake" in Spanish, and they're a staple in Mexico, other Latin American countries, and the southwestern United States. But if you ever happen to be in Spain, or in a Spanish restaurant, don't expect to be served these flatbreads if you order a tortilla: in Spanish cuisine, a tortilla is actually a savory, pan-cooked cake made of potatoes and eggs, similar to an omelet or an Italian frittata.

The true Mexican tortilla, however, is descended from a flatbread that's been made since 10,000 BC. Legend has it that the first tortilla was made by a Mayan peasant for his hungry king, and he created the dough from dried corn kernels. To make a finer flour for tortillas, the Mayans discovered that they could soak maize (corn), in an alkaline solution to remove the skins from the kernels, a process that is still used today to make masa harina, the corn flour used for modern-day corn tortillas.

TORTILLA NUTRITION

Tortillas are relatively low in fat and calories per serving. They have a few more calories than a slice of white bread, but are similar to white bread in fat, carbohydrates, fiber, and protein. Here is a comparison of the nutritional profile of flour and corn tortillas:

Type of Tortilla	Flour (6-inch)	Corn (6-inch)
Calories	94	52
Total Fat	2 g	1 g
Cholesterol	0 mg	0 mg
Sodium	191 mg	11 mg
Carbohydrates	15 g	11 g
Dietary Fiber	1 g	2 g
Protein	2 g	1 g

source: NutritionData.com

When they arrived in the New World in 1519, Cortes and his conquistadores discovered that the Aztecs were making flatbread cakes from maize, which they called *tlaxcalli*, a native word that the Spanish settlers adapted into their own language as "tortilla." For centuries, the tortillas were made by hand, and young women learned the precise techniques of grinding the corn, mixing it with water, patting it flat, and cooking it on hot stones. Later, tortillas were cooked on comals, Mexican stovetop griddles. Eventually tools were developed to make tortillas easier to prepare, such as wooden or metal hand-operated tortilla presses. And since the 1940s, automated machines have been developed to grind the corn and press and cook the tortillas for more efficient, larger-scale production. But even today, some *abuelas* still make tortillas by hand, and you might be able to peek into the kitchen of authentic Mexican restaurants to see the cooks pressing balls of dough flat and cooking them on griddles.

Tortillas are more popular in the U.S. than any other ethnic breads such as bagels, English muffins, and pita. Refrigerated commercial tortillas account for more than $248 million in sales, according to *Snack Food & Wholesale Bakery,* June 2011. The Tortilla Industry Association estimates total tortilla sales as more than $6 billion annually.

In old Mexico, tortillas were—and still are—used as an eating utensil, a habit picked up by Western cowboys, who discovered the convenience of filling tortillas with meat to make an easy dinner around the campfire. The American settlers of the Southwest, as well as Mexican immigrants to the U.S., helped tortillas gain a place in American cooking, and today it's hard to imagine our nation without Tex-Mex, Southwestern, and New Mexican cuisines, all of which include tortillas as an important component.

Homemade tortillas are delicious (try making them yourself using the recipes on page 191), but they require a bit of effort, not to mention some practice to get the tortillas thin enough. I'll make them from scratch if I have time or for a special occasion, but most of the time I keep my fridge stocked with bags of commercial tortillas. In most major cities, you can find tortillas made fresh by local factories.

Buying and Storing Tortillas

While tortillas were originally only made of corn, today you can find them in many varieties, flavors, and sizes. Commercial tortillas can be as small as 6 inches or as large as 10 or 12 inches. You might see them flavored with sun-dried tomatoes, herbs, garlic, chipotle peppers, and more. In the Southwest, you can find blue corn

> Tortillas are the #2-selling bread product in the U.S., after white bread.

tortillas, which have a stunning dark-blue color and a slightly nutty flavor.

Corn tortillas are generally found only in 6-inch sizes, as they're more fragile than their flour counterparts. True corn tortillas have the advantage of being gluten-free, but some commercial varieties are made with a combination of corn and wheat flours, so those who are gluten intolerant should double-check the label or call the manufacturer to make sure.

Flour tortillas contain gluten, which makes them more flexible and elastic. You can find small taco sizes or larger sizes to use for burritos or wrap sandwiches.

Store tortillas wrapped in the plastic bag they came in, in the refrigerator. Stored this way, they can keep for as long as several weeks. Most tortilla packages have an expiration date that can help you gauge whether they're still good. As long as they're still flexible and not hardened, and don't have signs of mold, they should be fine to eat. Even if they're a bit stiff, they will generally soften a bit when they're heated.

A genre of fine art, tortilla art uses baked tortillas, coated with acrylic, as a canvas for paintings. One of the leading tortilla artists, Los Angeles–based Joe Bravo, claims he began using tortillas when he didn't have money for actual canvases, while others use tortillas in art as a nod to their Latino heritage. Bravo has been commissioned to create tortilla art for celebrities like Tyra Banks and Hilary Duff.

Warming Tortillas

Although tortillas can be eaten straight from the package, either refrigerated or at room temperature, warming them up can make them more flexible, which means they're easier to fold and roll, and just generally makes them more appealing to eat. There are several ways you can warm up a tortilla to use in a rolled recipe or just to stuff with your favorite fillings.

In the Microwave: On a plate or a paper towel, stack the number of tortillas you need (5 at a time, maximum) and microwave on high power for 15 to 20 seconds until warmed and flexible. To prevent flour tortillas from drying out, you can loosely fold them in half and wrap them in a dry or dampened paper towel before putting them in the microwave.

On the Stove: There are three basic methods for warming tortillas on the stove—two for flour tortillas, and one for corn tortillas.

Method #1 (flour tortillas): Turn a gas burner on medium heat. Let the burner grate heat up for a moment or two, then lay the tortilla directly on the grate. Warm the tortilla for about 10 seconds, then carefully flip over with your fingers or tongs. Heat the tortilla until it's lightly browned and flexible. Keep the tortillas warm wrapped in a clean dishtowel as you're heating the number that you need.

Method #2 (flour tortillas): Heat a dry skillet over medium heat for a few moments until the pan is hot. Place a tortilla in the pan, heat for 15 to 20 seconds, and use tongs or a turning spatula to turn the tortilla over. Continue warming, flipping back and forth to heat evenly, until the tortilla is lightly golden and flexible. Keep the tortillas warm wrapped in a clean dishtowel as you're heating the number that you need.

Method #3 (corn tortillas): Brush a small skillet lightly with cooking oil, such as vegetable oil, and heat over medium heat. Add the tortilla and warm in the skillet for about 30 seconds, turning over to heat evenly, until the tortilla is flexible.

Keep tortillas warm wrapped in a clean dishtowel as you're heating the number that you need.

In the Oven: Preheat the oven to 250°F. Stack the tortillas and wrap loosely in aluminum foil. Place the packet on a baking sheet and heat in the oven for about 15 minutes, or until the middle of the stack is warmed through. This is the best way to heat up large quantities of tortillas at once—you can make individual packets of around 10 tortillas at a time, heat multiple packets at once, and leave the tortillas wrapped in the foil to stay warm.

On the Grill: If you're using an outdoor grill to make grilled fajitas, carne adovada (grilled beef), or other foods with which to fill your tortillas, you can warm flour tortillas right on the grill. Heat the grill to medium-hot. For flour tortillas, place the tortillas right on the grill grate and heat for 30 seconds, or until lightly browned. Turn over and heat an additional 30 seconds.

For corn tortillas, stack the tortillas (no more than 10 at a time) and wrap loosely in aluminum foil. Put the packet on a hot grill and heat for 5 to 10 minutes, turning over after 3 to 5 minutes to avoid burning the underside, until the middle tortillas are warmed through. Tortillas can be kept wrapped in the foil to stay warm. The foil-packet method also works for flour tortillas if you want to make a bunch at a time on the grill.

Fried: Frying corn tortillas in oil is a good way to cook corn tortillas for tostadas or flat enchiladas. In a small skillet, heat about ½ inch of vegetable oil until it shimmers. Add a tortilla (it should sizzle when a corner is dipped into the oil) and fry on one side until the underside is crisp, 25 to 30 seconds. Turn over and fry on the second side for another 25 to 30 seconds. Repeat with the desired number of tortillas. Drain tortillas on a paper towel–lined plate.

Getting Creative with Tortillas

In this book, you'll find tortillas being used in chip form or baked into cups. Here are the basic instructions to make cups, chips, and shells.

Baked Tortilla Chips: Preheat the oven to 375°F. Brush flour tortillas lightly with olive oil or vegetable oil on both sides. Cut into 8 wedges each and arrange on a baking sheet. Sprinkle with salt. Bake until they begin to get crispy, about 8 minutes, then turn the chips over and bake until crisp and lightly browned, 8 to 10 minutes longer. Let cool completely before serving or storing.

NASA has used flour tortillas instead of crumbly, perishable bread as food on space shuttle missions since the 1980s. The tortillas are easier to make a sandwich with than bread, and on longer missions will stay fresh longer. According to NASA, one of the astronauts' favorite meals in space is fajitas.

Fried Corn Tortilla Chips: Line a baking sheet with paper towels. Cut corn tortillas into wedges with a knife or a pizza cutter. Heat about 1 inch of vegetable oil in a medium saucepan to 350 to 375°F when checked with a candy or frying thermometer. Check that the oil is ready by dipping one piece of tortilla into the hot oil; it should bubble if it's hot enough.

Working in batches to avoid overcrowding, fry the tortilla wedges in the oil, turning over with a slotted spoon to cook evenly, about 1 minute for lightly crisped chips, or up to 2 minutes for a crunchier chip. Remove with a slotted spoon and spread the fried chips on the prepared baking sheet. Sprinkle immediately with salt or desired seasoning.

Tortilla Cups: Preheat the oven to 375°F. Warm a stack of 6-inch flour tortillas in the microwave for 15 seconds, or until flexible. Prick the tortillas all over with a fork. Brush both sides of the tortillas with melted butter or vegetable or olive oil. Fit the tortillas into small ovenproof bowls or ramekins, about 5 inches in diameter, or in muffin tins, crimping the sides of the tortillas loosely to fit them into the bowls. Bake for about 10 minutes or until the tortillas hold their shape on their own. Remove them from the bowls and finish baking on a sheet pan or directly on the oven rack until the tortillas are crisp and just beginning to brown, 5 to 10 minutes longer. Let cool completely.

Crispy Taco Shells (fried): Fill a skillet with about 1 inch of vegetable oil and heat the oil until it's shimmering. Place a corn tortilla in the hot oil (it should sizzle upon contact with the oil) and fry for about 15 seconds. Using tongs, fold the tortilla in half and use the tongs to hold the bottom side of the shell under the oil for about 15 seconds to allow it to get crisp and golden. Turn the entire folded tortilla over and hold the other side under the hot oil for another 15 seconds to cook evenly. Drain briefly on paper towels and fill and serve while still hot.

BREAKFASTS

From grab-and-go breakfast burritos to huevos rancheros, tortillas are often found on breakfast and brunch menus. But have you considered incorporating them into your breakfast routine at home? In my household, they're served alongside eggs more frequently than toast. Take a look at these recipes, which range from traditional to creative, and you too will say good-bye to boring old toast!

MIGAS

In parts of the Southwest, migas are ubiquitous on breakfast menus as
a way of using up leftover tortillas or chips from the previous night's
dinner, but I first had them at a little restaurant in the West Village
in New York. I loved the way the tortillas were softened by the eggs and
how the spicy jalapeños were cooled by a generous dollop of sour cream.
Now I order them whenever I see them on a brunch menu. They're not
much more complicated to make at home than a pan of scrambled eggs,
so don't feel like you have to wait until you find a place that serves
them. **Serves 4**

1 tablespoon vegetable oil

1 small onion, diced

6 small (6-inch) corn tortillas,
cut into strips

1 medium globe tomato, diced

6 large eggs

¾ cup shredded Colby Jack
cheese (2¾ ounces)

*Toppings: pickled jalapeños, chopped cilantro, sour cream,
diced avocado*

1. In a large nonstick skillet, heat the vegetable oil over medium-
high heat. Add the onion and the tortilla strips and cook, stirring
frequently, until the onions are translucent and the tortillas are
golden, about 8 minutes. Add the tomato and cook until the
tomato is softened and giving off its juice, about 2 minutes.

2. Whisk the eggs in a medium bowl. Reduce the heat to
medium-low and add the eggs to the pan. Cook, stirring, until
the eggs are scrambled, 2 to 3 minutes. Remove from the heat

and sprinkle the cheese over the eggs, stirring gently to combine. Let sit until melted. To serve, divide the *migas* among four plates and let everyone add the toppings of their choice.

· · · · · · · · ·

EGG AND SAUSAGE ROLL-UP

For an easy breakfast that's far more satisfying than a bowl of cereal and doesn't take much more time, try this quick scramble tucked into a tortilla. **Serves 2**

1 tablespoon unsalted butter

4 breakfast sausage patties chopped into chunks (about 8 ounces)

4 large eggs

½ cup shredded Colby cheese (2 ounces)

2 medium (8-inch) flour tortillas

hot sauce

kosher salt and black pepper

1. Melt the butter in a small nonstick skillet over medium heat. Add the sausage and cook, stirring occasionally with a rubber spatula, until cooked through, 5 to 7 minutes. Reduce the heat to medium-low. Lightly whisk the eggs in a small bowl, then add them to the pan. Cook, stirring frequently, until the eggs are no longer liquid but are still soft. Season lightly with salt and pepper. Sprinkle the eggs with the cheese, remove from the heat, and allow the cheese to melt.

2. Over an open burner, heat the tortillas until warm and softened, about 20 seconds on each side. Place the tortillas on two plates and divide the egg mixture between them. Roll the tortillas around the eggs. Season to taste with hot sauce and serve immediately.

· · · · · · · · ·

BACON, EGG, AND CHEESE ROLL

At the famous Tia Sophia's restaurant in Santa Fe, this is my favorite breakfast to order. I'm not sure why, since it's such a simple concept: scrambled eggs, a thick slab of bacon, and a sprinkling of cheese folded up in a flour tortilla. I particularly like asking for a side of red chile sauce to drizzle over it, but a spoonful of salsa also adds nice flavor.

Serves 2

4 slices thick-cut bacon

4 large eggs

2 medium (8-inch) flour tortillas

½ cup shredded Monterey Jack cheese (2 ounces)

kosher salt and black pepper

prepared salsa, red chile sauce, or enchilada sauce, to serve (optional)

1. Place the bacon in a small nonstick skillet and cook over medium-high heat, turning over when the underside is cooked, 5 to 7 minutes total. While the bacon is cooking, lightly beat the eggs in a small bowl. Transfer the bacon to a plate and keep warm under aluminum foil. Drain the excess oil from the pan. Reduce the heat to medium-low. Add the eggs and cook over medium-low heat, stirring constantly, until the eggs are cooked but still soft, about 5 minutes. Season to taste with salt and pepper.

2. Warm the tortillas in the microwave or over an open burner. To serve, place 2 pieces of bacon in the center of each tortilla. Divide the scrambled eggs between the tortillas, and sprinkle with the cheese. Serve with salsa, chile sauce, or enchilada sauce, if desired.

• • • • • • • • •

THE ULTIMATE BREAKFAST BURRITO

My husband's favorite breakfast is probably a breakfast burrito stuffed with all sorts of goodies. In Santa Fe, they nearly always have seasoned potatoes inside, which makes them more substantial. A breakfast burrito is a great way to use up leftovers from meals during the week, such as cheese, cooked vegetables, leftover salsa or enchilada sauce, or beans. **Serves 2**

4 slices bacon

1 medium russet potato, peeled and cut into ¾-inch cubes

1 (15-ounce) can pinto or black beans, undrained

1 tablespoon unsalted butter

4 large eggs

2 large (10 to 12-inch) flour tortillas

½ cup shredded Colby or Monterey Jack cheese (2 ounces)

¼ cup prepared salsa

kosher salt and black pepper

1. Place the bacon in a large nonstick skillet. Heat the pan over medium-high heat and cook the bacon, turning when crisp on the underside, until cooked through and crisp, 5 to 7 minutes. Transfer the bacon to a plate. Drain all but 1 tablespoon excess oil from the pan.

2. Add the potatoes and cook, stirring and turning occasionally, until browned and tender throughout, about 10 minutes. Transfer the potatoes to a plate or a bowl and cover with aluminum foil to keep warm. While potatoes are cooking, warm the beans in a small saucepan over medium-low heat.

3. Melt the butter in the pan over medium-low heat, tilting to coat the pan's surface. Lightly beat the eggs in a small bowl with a fork. Pour the eggs into the pan and cook, stirring occasionally, until the eggs are cooked through but still soft, 3 to 5 minutes.

4. To assemble the burritos, warm the tortillas in the microwave on high power for 15 to 20 seconds or over an open burner for about 10 seconds on each side. Divide the eggs between the tortillas, and top each with 2 slices of bacon, half the potatoes, ¼ to ½ cup beans, half the cheese, and half the salsa. Wrap like a burrito (see page 75) and serve.

• • • • • • • •

EGG IN A HOLE

One of my family's favorite camping breakfasts is eggs in a hole—we toast bread on a camp-stove griddle, cut a hole in the middle, and break an egg into it to fry. My friend Kelley wondered if something similar might work with tortillas, and I was up to the challenge. **Serves 4**

1 (14-ounce) can black beans, drained and rinsed

2 cups shredded Monterey Jack cheese (8 ounces)

8 medium (8-inch) flour tortillas

2 tablespoons unsalted butter, or more as needed

4 large eggs

kosher salt and black pepper

1. Divide the black beans and cheese among 4 tortillas and top each with a second tortilla to form quesadillas. Spray a medium nonstick skillet with cooking spray and heat it over medium-high heat. Reduce the heat to medium, place a quesadilla in the skillet, and cook until the underside is lightly browned and the cheese inside begins to melt, 2 to 3 minutes. Flip the quesadilla over and cook until the second side is lightly browned and the cheese is melted, 2 to 3 minutes longer. Remove the quesadilla to a cutting board and repeat with the remaining quesadillas. Use a 3-inch round biscuit cutter or a paring knife to cut a hole in the center of each quesadilla.

2. Return 1 quesadilla to the pan, still over medium heat, and place a small dab of butter on the pan in the center of the hole. When the butter melts, carefully break an egg into the hole. Let cook until the white is completely set and the yolk is cooked to your liking. Season with a sprinkle each of salt and pepper. Repeat with the remaining quesadillas and eggs. Serve hot.

• • • • • • • • •

SMOKED SALMON AND EGG STACKERS

Smoked salmon, goat cheese, and dill are classic fancy-breakfast fare. But you don't need a special occasion, or even a lot of time, to make this delicious and rich breakfast. Serve this up for a romantic breakfast for two, complete with fun coffee drinks and a platter of fresh fruit.

Serves 2

2 ounces goat cheese, softened

2 teaspoons minced fresh dill or chives, plus 2 sprigs for garnish

4 small (6-inch) flour tortillas

1 tablespoon unsalted butter

4 large eggs

3 ounces smoked salmon, chopped

kosher salt and black pepper

1. In a small bowl, mix the goat cheese with the dill or chives. Slightly warm the tortillas over an open burner or in a dry skillet, about 20 seconds per side. Spread the goat cheese mixture on the tortillas and set aside.

2. Melt the butter in a small nonstick skillet over medium-low heat. Lightly beat the eggs in a small bowl with a fork or a whisk. Pour the eggs into the skillet and cook, stirring frequently with a rubber spatula, until the eggs are no longer liquid but are still soft and creamy. Stir in the salmon.

3. To serve, place 2 prepared tortillas on each of two plates. Spread a scoop of the eggs on 1 tortilla, top with the second tortilla, and spread the remaining egg mixture on top. Garnish with a sprig of chives or dill, if desired. Serve immediately.

· · · · · · · · ·

AVOCADO AND LEEK OMELET WRAP

Wrapping a flour tortilla around an omelet makes it a bit more portable and adds some substance. I love the way the chunks of avocado get creamy and melty within their warm egg wrapping. This is a great grab-and-go breakfast for a morning commute. **Serves 1**

2 teaspoons extra-virgin olive oil

½ leek, chopped

2 large eggs

2 tablespoons milk

1 tablespoon unsalted butter

¼ cup shredded Monterey Jack cheese (1 ounce)

½ medium avocado, diced

1 medium (8-inch) flour tortilla

kosher salt and black pepper

1. In a small nonstick skillet, heat the olive oil over medium heat. Add the leek and cook, stirring occasionally with a rubber spatula, until softened and translucent, about 5 minutes. Transfer to a small bowl or plate and set aside.

2. In a small bowl, whisk together the eggs and the milk. Melt the butter in the skillet over medium-low heat, tilting to coat the surface completely. Pour the eggs into the skillet, tilting to spread the eggs evenly over the entire pan. Let the eggs cook, undisturbed, until the eggs are set and only a little liquid remains in the center. As the egg is cooking, warm the tortilla over an open burner or in the microwave and place on a plate. Sprinkle the cheese and avocado in a strip along the center of the omelet. Season the entire omelet lightly with salt and pepper. With the spatula, carefully fold one side of the omelet, and then the other, over the filling. Slide the rolled omelet onto the tortilla and roll the tortilla around the omelet. Serve immediately.

• • • • • • • •

NEW MEXICAN BENEDICTS

For a brunch party or a lazy Sunday morning, nothing beats eggs Benedict. In this version, the classic Benedict ingredient of Canadian bacon gets tucked into a quesadilla, and the hollandaise sauce is infused with Southwestern zest thanks to cumin and lime juice. You can make the hollandaise sauce a little bit in advance; it'll keep in the double boiler over hot water for at least an hour, and if it thickens, you can add a little hot water to return it to a pourable consistency.

Serves 4

juice of ½ lime, divided (about 2 tablespoons)

¼ teaspoon kosher salt

4 large egg yolks

½ cup (1 stick) unsalted butter, melted

⅛ teaspoon ground cumin

1 teaspoon canola oil

3 ounces Canadian bacon, diced

8 small (6-inch) flour tortillas

1 cup shredded Monterey Jack cheese (4 ounces)

1 tablespoon white vinegar

4 large eggs

2 tablespoons chopped fresh cilantro, for garnish

1. To make the hollandaise sauce, pour water into the bottom of a double boiler and bring to a simmer. If you don't have a double boiler, fit a heatproof bowl, such as stainless steel, over a pan with 1 to 2 inches of water in it (the water should not touch the bottom of the bowl), and bring to a simmer. Place 1 tablespoon lime juice and the salt in the double boiler and whisk to combine and dissolve the salt. Add the egg yolks and whisk constantly until the yolks have thickened and increased in volume, 7 to 9 minutes. Remove from the heat and gradually whisk in the melted butter in a steady, thin stream until all the butter is incorporated and the sauce is smooth. Whisk in the remaining lime juice and the cumin, and season to taste with additional salt as needed. Cover the bowl with plastic wrap and leave sitting over the hot water, off the burner.

2. To make the quesadillas, preheat the oven to the warm setting, about 170°F. In a small nonstick skillet, heat the canola oil over medium-high heat. Add the Canadian bacon and cook, stirring occasionally, until the bacon is heated and slightly crisp, about 5 minutes. Set 4 tortillas on a work surface and sprinkle them with the cheese. Divide the bacon among the tortillas, sprinkling evenly over the cheese. Place the remaining 4 tortillas on top to make quesadillas. One at a time, cook the quesadillas in the skillet, until the tortillas are toasted and the cheese is melted, 1 to 2 minutes on each side. Keep the quesadillas warm on a baking sheet in the oven.

3. Fill a medium saucepan with about 3 inches of water and stir in the vinegar. Bring the water to a simmer. Carefully break an egg into the water (or break it into a small bowl and then slip the egg from the bowl into the pan for more control). Use a slotted spoon to keep the white from spreading. Break the remaining eggs into the pan (or work in batches if they don't all fit). Let cook, undisturbed, until the white is completely set but the yolk still yields slightly to the touch, 3 to 5 minutes.

4. To assemble the Benedicts, place a quesadilla on a plate. If the hollandaise sauce is too thick, stir in a few tablespoons of the egg poaching water. Remove a poached egg from the pan with a slotted spoon and, if desired, use a paper towel to lightly pat it dry of excess water. Place the egg in the center of the quesadilla. Drizzle some of the hollandaise sauce over the egg and the tortilla. Garnish with cilantro. Repeat with the remaining ingredients and serve.

● ● ● ● ● ● ● ●

TORTILLA-CRUSTED FRENCH TOAST

Leftover tortilla chips, whether homemade or store-bought, add fun to basic French toast. If you love salty-sweet combinations, you'll love the juxtaposition of salted chips against a generous drizzle of maple syrup. But if that sounds a little too crazy for breakfast, seek out unsalted chips. My favorite bread for French toast is a crusty artisan loaf, such as a boule or a wide French loaf. Cut it into thick slices, about 1½ inches wide, and set the slices out on the counter the night before to dry out so that they can better absorb the egg custard. **Serves 4**

2 large eggs

1 cup whole milk

1 teaspoon vanilla extract

pinch kosher salt

8 cups tortilla chips (4 to 5 ounces)

2 tablespoons brown sugar

1 teaspoon ground cinnamon

unsalted butter, for griddle

8 slices slightly stale bread

maple syrup, to serve

1. Whisk the eggs in a shallow bowl. Whisk in the milk, vanilla, and salt until smooth. Set aside.

2. Finely crush the tortilla chips in a food processor or in a large zip-top bag. Add the brown sugar and cinnamon, and shake the bag or pulse the food processor to combine. Transfer the tortilla chip mixture to a shallow bowl or a pie pan.

3. Melt about 1 tablespoon butter on a griddle or nonstick pan over medium-high heat. Dip 1 slice of bread in the egg mixture, letting it soak for a moment and turning to coat completely.

Then place the bread in the tortilla crumbs, sprinkle a handful of crumbs over the top, and lightly press the crumbs into the bread to help them adhere. Place the crusted bread on the griddle or pan, working in batches to avoid overcrowding. Cook on one side until the tortilla crust begins to brown and the egg mixture is no longer liquid, about 4 minutes. Flip the French toast over and cook another 4 minutes on the second side. Keep the cooked French toast warm in a warm oven (170°F) or under aluminum foil while you make the rest, using more butter as needed for the cooking surface. Serve warm with maple syrup.

• • • • • • • • •

SHORTCUT BLINTZES

On my father's side, I have a Jewish–Eastern European background, so growing up we occasionally enjoyed blintzes for brunch or even dinner as a special treat. Making the crêpelike pancakes for them, however, is time-consuming and delicate. While flour tortillas don't have the same delicate texture of the traditional pancakes, you won't notice too much of a difference, and these are so much easier to make! **Serves 4 (makes 8 blintzes)**

1½ tablespoons unsalted butter, melted, divided

2 cups cottage cheese

½ cup mascarpone or cream cheese

¼ cup confectioners' sugar

½ teaspoon ground cinnamon

8 small (6-inch) flour tortillas

1 (21-ounce) can cherry or blueberry pie filling

1. Preheat the oven to 350°F. Lightly brush an 11 x 7-inch or 9 x 13-inch glass baking dish with about ½ tablespoon of the melted butter.

2. In the jar of a blender, combine the cottage cheese, mascarpone or cream cheese, confectioners' sugar, and cinnamon. Blend until smooth. Spread about ¼ cup filling on each tortilla and roll the tortillas. Arrange the tortillas in the prepared baking dish seam-side down to keep them from unrolling. Brush the tortillas with the remaining 1 tablespoon melted butter. Bake until the tortillas start to turn light golden and the filling is warmed through, about 15 minutes.

3. While the blintzes are baking, warm the pie filling in a small saucepan over medium-low heat. To serve, place 2 blintzes on each plate and top with a spoonful of filling. Serve warm.

• • • • • • • • •

YOGURT PARFAITS IN TORTILLA CUPS

These parfaits make a fun breakfast for kids or a pretty presentation for a brunch. You can get creative with the fruits you use—try other berries like raspberries or blackberries, or diced peaches, kiwi, or plums.

Serves 6

2 teaspoons ground cinnamon

1 tablespoon sugar

6 medium (8-inch) flour tortillas

2 tablespoons unsalted butter, melted

24 ounces vanilla or plain yogurt

1 cup fresh blueberries

1 cup diced fresh strawberries

honey, for garnish

1. Preheat the oven to 375°F. In a small bowl, mix the cinnamon and the sugar. Brush the tortillas on both sides with the melted butter and sprinkle with the cinnamon-sugar. Stack the tortillas and microwave on high power until soft, about 15 seconds. Carefully crimp the tortillas to fit into the cups of a standard muffin pan, using your fingers to push the tortillas so that they form to the base of the pan. Bake the tortillas until they're crisp and hold their shape, about 15 minutes. Let cool.

2. To make the parfaits, spoon a little yogurt into the base of each tortilla cup. Sprinkle with a layer of fruit. Top with additional layers of yogurt and fruit. Drizzle with honey. Serve immediately.

· · · · · · · · ·

STARTERS
and SNACKS

Go beyond the traditional party snack of chips and dips with these more innovative recipes. After all, everyone loves snacking on tortillas, but their appetites will be whetted all the more if the tortilla is filled with something tasty, from rich and indulgent bacon and horseradish to Asian-inspired seasoned pork in a mock wonton.

MEXICALI ROLL-UPS

My friend Kevyn throws a heck of a party, and these easy appetizers are one of his standbys. You can assemble them in advance and then bake them as guests are arriving. This is a forgiving recipe; you can customize the roll-ups with different fillings, such as ground beef, fresh cilantro, different kinds of cheeses, or pickled jalapeños. Just be sure to chop up the ingredients so you can roll them tightly. If you're preparing these in advance (up to one day), at the end of Step 2, tightly roll each tortilla in plastic wrap and refrigerate until needed. **Makes about 40 pieces**

1 (16-ounce) can refried beans

½ teaspoon ground cumin

2 tablespoons prepared salsa

4 large (10 to 12-inch) flour tortillas

¼ cup sour cream

1 cup shredded Colby Jack cheese (4 ounces)

1 (4-ounce) can sliced black olives

4 scallions, chopped

1. Preheat the oven to 350°F. Line a rimmed baking sheet with aluminum foil and spray the foil with cooking spray.

2. In a medium bowl, combine the refried beans with the cumin and salsa, and stir until smooth. Divide the bean mixture among the tortillas, spreading in an even layer over each tortilla, leaving about 1 inch uncovered on one side. Spread about 1 tablespoon of sour cream over the beans. Sprinkle each with cheese, black olives, and scallions. Beginning with one end, roll the tortillas tightly but without squeezing the ingredients out.

3. Place each rolled tortilla on the prepared baking sheet seam-side down. Bake until the tortillas are lightly browned, 10 to 15 minutes. Let cool on the baking sheet for 5 minutes, then transfer to a cutting board and slice crosswise into 1-inch pieces with a sharp serrated knife. Serve warm.

. . . .

CREAMY BACON AND HORSERADISH WEDGES

These easy-to-make appetizers have a lot of complexity flavor-wise: There's the salty smokiness of the bacon, the creaminess of the cream cheese, the heat of the horseradish, and the slight bitterness of the arugula. Put it all together and it makes for an addictive party snack.

Makes 12 wedges

3 slices crispy cooked bacon, crumbled

⅓ cup cream cheese

1 teaspoon prepared horseradish

3 small (6-inch) flour tortillas

¾ cup baby arugula (about ¾ ounce)

1. In a small bowl, stir together the bacon, cream cheese, and horseradish until combined. Evenly spread the cream cheese mixture among the tortillas. Place about ¼ cup of arugula on one half of each tortilla and fold the tortillas in half over the arugula and cream cheese filling, pressing down slightly to seal.

2. Heat a medium nonstick skillet over medium heat. Place as many of the filled tortillas as will fit in the pan and cook until the underside is golden and the filling warmed, about 2 minutes. Flip the tortillas over and cook on the second side until browned, about 2 minutes longer. Place on a cutting board and cut each into 4 wedges. Serve warm.

. . . .

SPINACH AND CHEESE EMPANADAS

When you don't feel like dealing with fussy pastry dough, just fold a flour tortilla around a filling and bake. It makes a light, crisp crust for empanadas and other filled pastries. These empanadas are fairly large, so if you're planning the menu for a party, you'll probably only need one per guest. **Makes 8 empanadas**

1 (16-ounce) bag frozen chopped spinach, thawed

½ cup cottage cheese

¾ cup grated Jarlsberg cheese

½ teaspoon kosher salt

⅛ teaspoon black pepper

1 large egg

8 small (6-inch) flour tortillas

1. Preheat the oven to 375°F. Squeeze the excess water from the spinach. In a large bowl, stir together the spinach, cottage cheese, Jarlsberg cheese, salt, and pepper. In a small bowl, lightly beat the egg with a fork.

2. Mound about 2 tablespoons of spinach mixture to one side of the center of a tortilla. With a pastry brush, brush the edges of the tortilla with egg. Fold the tortilla in half over the filling to make a half-circle shape. Press lightly on the middle of the empanadas to push out any air pockets, then press down very firmly along the edges to seal the tortilla closed. Repeat with the remaining tortillas and place the finished empanadas on a baking sheet. Brush the tops of each empanada with beaten egg and, with a sharp paring knife, cut one or two slits in the top of each empanada to allow steam to vent. Bake until the tortillas are crisp, about 15 minutes. Serve warm or at room temperature.

• • • • • • • •

CHORIZO AND
COJACK TAQUITOS

Taquitos are quintessential festival food in the Southwest, particularly in Santa Fe, where you can find them at fiestas, rodeos, carnivals, and other public events. Normally they're deep-fried and as skinny as cigars, but I've opted to bake my version to make them a little healthier and easier to prepare. That doesn't make them any less delicious, in my opinion. For a party, you could either serve them whole or cut them in halves or quarters for an easier to eat, bite-size nibble. Unlike Spanish chorizo, which is cured and more like a hard sausage, Mexican chorizo is usually found fresh (uncooked), in links. **Makes 6 taquitos**

8 ounces Mexican chorizo (about 2½ links), casings removed

1½ cups shredded Colby Jack cheese (6 ounces)

6 small (6-inch) flour tortillas

1 tablespoon vegetable oil

1. Preheat the oven to 450°F. In a medium nonstick skillet over TK heat, cook the chorizo, breaking it into smaller pieces with a spatula, until browned and cooked through, 5 to 7 minutes. Transfer the chorizo to a plate with a slotted spoon, allowing excess fat to drain back into the pan.

2. Stack the tortillas and microwave on high power until pliable, about 20 seconds. Cover all but one tortilla with a clean dishtowel. Sprinkle the tortilla with about 2 tablespoons cheese, leaving about 1 inch uncovered on one side. Sprinkle about 1 tablespoon chorizo over the cheese. Roll the tortilla tightly, ending with the uncovered end and being careful not to squeeze the filling out. Place the tortilla seam-side down on a baking sheet. Repeat with the remaining ingredients. Brush the rolled taquitos lightly with vegetable oil. Bake until golden and crisp, 12 to 15 minutes. Serve hot or warm.

· · · · · · · · ·

BAKED WONTONS WITH SWEET-AND-SOUR DIPPING SAUCE

Flour tortillas are pretty similar to the flat pancakes used in Chinese dishes like wontons and mu shu, so you need not feel like any recipe you make with tortillas has to have a Mexican flavor to it. In this recipe, ground pork is seasoned with ginger, soy sauce, and hoisin to make an Asian filling for baked wontons. These make a delicious party food, a fun starter, or a side dish to a stir-fry dinner. **Makes 16 wontons**

2 teaspoons plus 1 tablespoon vegetable oil, divided

3 scallions, chopped

12 ounces ground pork

2 tablespoons soy sauce

1 tablespoon minced fresh ginger

2 tablespoons hoisin sauce

8 small (6-inch) flour tortillas, halved

2 tablespoons sesame seeds

½ cup prepared sweet-and-sour sauce, to serve

1. Preheat the oven to 375°F. Heat 2 teaspoons of the vegetable oil in a medium nonstick skillet. Add the scallions and cook, stirring occasionally, until softened, 3 to 4 minutes. Add the pork and cook, breaking the meat into small chunks with a wooden spoon or spatula, until cooked through, 7 to 8 minutes. Stir in the soy sauce, ginger, and hoisin sauce. Remove from the heat.

2. Fill a small bowl with warm water and have on hand near your work surface. Spoon about 1 tablespoon of the pork mixture into the middle of a tortilla half. Using your finger, brush water along the edge of the tortilla. Fold the tortilla in half to make a triangle and press the edges firmly together, squeezing to seal the tortilla closed over the filling. Repeat with the remaining tortilla halves and filling.

3. Place the wontons on a baking sheet and use a pastry brush to brush the tops with the remaining 1 tablespoon vegetable oil. Sprinkle the wontons with the sesame seeds. Bake until crisp, about 20 minutes. Serve with sweet-and-sour sauce for dipping.

• • • • • • • •

SPIKED GAZPACHO DIP WITH SEASONED TORTILLA CHIPS

Gazpacho, a Spanish chilled soup, is so refreshing on a hot day. With its tomato base, though, it always reminds me of salsa, which inspired me to dream up this dip. The splash of tequila makes this a decidedly grown-up snack, but you can always omit the booze or set aside part of the dip for teetotalers and kids. **Serves 8 to 10**

3 medium globe tomatoes, cored, quartered, and seeded

2 ribs celery, cut into large chunks

½ medium red onion, cut into large chunks

1 medium cucumber, peeled, seeded, and cut into large chunks

1 medium red or green bell pepper, seeded and cut into large chunks

juice of 1 lime (about 2 tablespoons)

1 teaspoon minced jalapeño

2 tablespoons fresh cilantro

2½ teaspoons kosher salt, divided

5 small (6-inch) flour tortillas

1 tablespoon canola oil

1 teaspoon chipotle powder

1 ounce white tequila

1. In a food processor, combine the tomatoes, celery, onion, cucumber, bell pepper, and lime juice. Pulse to process the vegetables into a chunky puree. Add the jalapeño, cilantro, and ½ teaspoon of the salt, and pulse to combine. Transfer to a container with a lid and refrigerate for 1 hour, or up to 1 day, to allow the flavors to meld.

2. To make the chips, preheat the oven to 375°F. Brush the tortillas on both sides with canola oil. Using a knife or a pizza wheel, cut the tortillas into wedges. Arrange the wedges on a rimmed baking sheet (use two sheets if they don't all fit) and sprinkle them on both sides with the chipotle powder and the remaining 2 teaspoons salt. Bake for 5 minutes, turn the chips over and bake until crisp, 5 to 7 minutes longer. If you're using two pans in the oven on two different racks, rotate the racks halfway through cooking. Allow the chips to cool completely on the pan.

3. Just before serving, transfer the gazpacho dip to a serving bowl. Drizzle with the tequila and stir to combine. Serve cold.

· · · · · · · · ·

NACHO BITES

I'm probably in the minority, but I'm not a fan of nachos, especially when I'm sharing a big plate of them. Inevitably, the first chips are almost too overloaded with the delicious toppings, and near the bottom, you're lucky if the remaining chips even have a shred or two of congealed cheese. This recipe is a bit labor intensive, but each bite is guaranteed to have just the right amount of toppings. **Serves 8 to 10**

1 (15-ounce) can refried beans

¼ cup prepared salsa

1 (9-ounce) bag tortilla chips or 1 recipe baked tortilla chips (see page 19)

2 cups shredded Colby cheese (8 ounces)

1 (6-ounce) container sour cream

1 (11-ounce) can pickled jalapeños, drained

2 scallions, chopped

1. Heat the beans and salsa in a small saucepan over medium heat, stirring occasionally to combine and warm through, about 5 minutes.

2. Preheat the oven's broiler. Place the sour cream in a piping bag or a zip-top bag with one corner cut off. Arrange the tortilla chips in a single layer on a baking sheet. Spoon about ½ tablespoon of bean mixture onto each chip, spreading the beans slightly but leaving a corner of the chip exposed for a "handle." Top the beans with a little cheese. Put the baking sheet under the broiler until the cheese starts to melt and bubble, about 3 minutes. Remove from the oven, let cool slightly, and then pipe a dollop of sour cream onto each chip. Garnish with a pickled jalapeño slice and a few scallion pieces. Serve warm.

• • • • • • • •

MEXICAN SNACK MIX

Bring a bowl of snack mix to a party and you can pretty much guarantee your bowl will be coming home empty. I adapted this version from the classic recipe that's on the back of cereals like Chex and Crispix, adding tortilla bits and some Southwestern flavors to give it a twist. **Makes 4½ cups**

3 cups Chex-style cereal, any variety or combination

1 cup roasted, salted shelled peanuts

½ cup small pretzel shapes

3 medium (8-inch) flour tortillas, cut into 1-inch squares

2 tablespoons unsalted butter

½ teaspoon ground cumin

¼ teaspoon garlic powder

¼ teaspoon kosher salt

¼ teaspoon red chile powder or ⅛ teaspoon cayenne pepper

1 tablespoon freshly squeezed lime juice

2 teaspoons Worcestershire sauce

1. Preheat the oven to 275°F. In a 9 x13-inch glass baking dish, combine the cereal, peanuts, pretzels, and tortillas. Use clean hands to toss the ingredients so they're evenly combined.

2. Melt the butter in a small microwave-safe bowl. Add the cumin, garlic powder, salt, chile powder, lime juice, and Worcestershire sauce. Stir with a fork to combine. Drizzle the butter mixture over the cereal mixture and use a large spoon or clean hands to toss to coat. Bake until the tortillas are crisp, stirring two or three times during the cooking time, about 45 minutes total. Serve at room temperature. Store for 1 to 2 days in an airtight container or a zip-top bag.

• • • • • • • • •

SOUPS, SALADS, and SIDES

Tortillas can add crunch, flavor, and visual appeal to a wide range of side dishes and light meals like soups. Whether it's baking a tortilla into a bowl and filling it, sprinkling the top of a dish with crunchy chips or baked strips, or even blending tortillas into a soup to give it texture and favor, tortillas can work in many ways to make delicious sides.

TORTILLA SOUP

Tortilla soup is like the Southwestern equivalent of chicken noodle soup, and no less restorative. I've sampled tortilla soups everywhere from hole-in-the-wall Mexican restaurants to Santa Fe's finest restaurants (where the server poured the soup tableside into my bowl, in which the tortilla strips were already artfully arranged). Every establishment has its own "secret recipe," but I think that a generous squeeze of lime, plenty of chicken chunks, and some perfectly ripe diced avocado to serve on top are all must-have ingredients. For the chicken, use any combination of breasts and thighs. **Serves 4**

1 tablespoon vegetable oil, plus more for frying

1 small yellow onion, diced

1 medium red bell pepper, diced

4 cups chicken broth

1 (15-ounce) can diced tomatoes

1½ cups frozen corn

1 pound boneless, skinless chicken, cut into 1-inch chunks

juice of 1 lime (about 2 tablespoons)

1 teaspoon ground cumin

3 small (6-inch) corn tortillas

kosher salt and black pepper

lime wedges, for garnish

diced avocado, for garnish

1. Heat the vegetable oil in a large Dutch oven over medium heat. Add the onion and bell pepper and cook, stirring occasionally, until very soft, 7 to 9 minutes. Add the chicken broth, tomatoes, and corn. Bring to a simmer, add the chicken, and reduce the heat to low or to maintain a simmer. Simmer, uncovered, until the chicken is cooked through, 20 to 25 minutes. Stir in the lime juice and cumin, and season to taste with salt and pepper.

2. While the chicken is cooking, heat about 1 inch of vegetable oil in a small saucepan until the oil is shimmering. Cut the tortillas in half, then cut the halves crosswise into ½-inch strips. Line a rimmed baking sheet with paper towels. Working in batches, fry the tortilla strips until crisp, about 1 minute, stirring to turn them over to fry evenly. Remove from the oil with a slotted spoon, letting excess oil drip back into the pan, then spread on the paper towels. Sprinkle generously with salt while hot.

3. To serve, ladle soup into individual bowls. Garnish with a lime wedge, a few pieces of diced avocado, and a little mound of tortilla strips in the center of each bowl.

• • • • • • • • •

BLACK BEAN SOUP IN TORTILLA BOWLS

This cute presentation serves up unctuous black bean soup in its own edible bowl. I love to break off chunks of the crunchy bowl for dipping. You can also make the bowls to serve chili or other thick soups, or even to use to hold dips like guacamole or bean dip. **Serves 4**

2 teaspoons vegetable oil

1 medium yellow onion, diced

2 ribs celery, diced

1 medium red bell pepper, diced

2 (15-ounce) cans black beans, undrained

1 cup vegetable broth

½ teaspoon ground cumin

¼ teaspoon kosher salt

2 tablespoons freshly squeezed lime juice

4 tortilla bowls (see page 58)

2 scallions, minced

1 medium avocado, diced

lime wedges, for garnish

1. In a large Dutch oven or a heavy soup pot, heat the vegetable oil over medium heat. Add the onion, celery, and bell pepper and cook, stirring occasionally, until softened, 7 to 9 minutes. Stir in the beans, vegetable broth, and cumin. Bring to a simmer, then reduce the heat to low, cover, and simmer until the vegetables are very soft and the flavors have had a chance to meld, about 20 minutes.

2. Ladle about 1½ cups of the soup into a bowl and puree with an immersion blender until mostly smooth (or transfer the 1½ cups of soup to a blender and puree). Return the pureed soup to the pot and stir to combine. Simmer, uncovered, until all the ingredients are tender and the soup is thick, 15 to 20 minutes longer. Stir in the lime juice and season to taste with more salt and cumin, if desired.

3. To serve, set a tortilla bowl on a small plate or shallow bowl. Spoon soup into the bowl and garnish with scallion, avocado, and a lime wedge.

. . . .

TORTILLA BOWLS

Use ramekins, ovenproof bowls, or individual cake pans to make bowls in a size you like. You can also find special pans for making tortilla bowls in kitchenware stores or online. Companies that make them include Norpro and Chicago Metallic.

4 medium (8-inch) flour tortillas
1 tablespoon vegetable oil
kosher salt

Preheat the oven to 375°F. Brush the tortillas on both sides with the vegetable oil and sprinkle with salt. Fit a tortilla into an ovenproof, flat-bottomed bowl, making sure to mold the tortilla to the bottom of the bowl so that it will have a flat base, and crimping the tortilla to fit the sides. Bake the tortilla in the bowl until it holds its shape on its own, about 10 minutes. Remove from the bowl and place the tortilla bowl directly on the oven rack or a baking sheet, and bake until crisp and just beginning to turn golden, 3 to 5 minutes longer. Remove from the oven and let cool before filling. Repeat with the remaining tortillas.

GREEN CHILE STEW WITH WARM TORTILLAS

This spicy stew is not for the faint of heart, although its level of spiciness depends on the heat of the chiles you use. Store-bought canned chiles don't have much heat, so I like to bring home frozen green chiles when I visit my mom in Santa Fe. You can order fresh and frozen green chiles online; one source is Berridge Farms (www.hatchnmgreenchile.com). This stew is traditionally served with flour tortillas, which can be dipped into the soup or even used to scoop up ingredients. I love thick, fresh homemade flour tortillas with this, but store-bought will work too, especially if they're lightly toasted over a burner until they're warm and soft. Pork shoulder is the best choice for the meat in this recipe. **Serves 6**

1 tablespoon vegetable oil

2 pounds boneless pork, cut into cubes

1 medium yellow onion, diced

2 cloves garlic, minced

3 tablespoons all-purpose flour

1 (28-ounce) can diced tomatoes

1 cup chicken broth

1 teaspoon dried oregano

½ teaspoon ground cumin

½ cup chopped roasted New Mexico green chiles, most seeds removed

6 small (6-inch) flour tortillas, warmed

kosher salt and black pepper

1. Heat the oil in a large Dutch oven or heavy soup pot over medium heat. Season the pork with salt and pepper and add to the pot. Cook, turning the pieces to cook evenly, until browned, about 6 minutes. Add the onions and cook, stirring occasionally, until the onions are translucent, about 5 minutes. Add the garlic and cook, stirring constantly, for 30 seconds. Sprinkle the flour over the ingredients in the pot and cook, stirring, until the flour forms a paste and browns lightly, about 1 minute.

2. Stir in the tomatoes, chicken broth, oregano, and cumin. Bring to a simmer and reduce the heat to low. Simmer, covered, for 45 minutes to allow the flavors to meld. Stir in the chiles and simmer, uncovered, until the chiles mellow and the soup is slightly thickened, about 30 seconds longer. Spoon into individual bowls and serve with warm tortillas to scoop up the stew.

. . . .

TOMATO SOUP WITH ASIAGO TORTILLA CRISPS

Out of bread one day, I made my kids quesadillas instead of grilled cheese sandwiches to go alongside bowls of tomato soup. They loved the combination and to this day it's a routine lunch at our house. I was inspired to make this dressier version that I could serve for a light dinner, alongside a salad. This recipe makes more tortilla crisps than you'll actually need for the meal, and for good reason—you won't be able to stop snacking on them when they come out of the oven!

Serves 6

2 tablespoons unsalted butter

1 medium yellow onion, diced

2 ribs celery, diced

2 medium carrots, peeled and diced

1 medium red bell pepper, minced

1 large clove garlic, minced

1 (28-ounce) can diced tomatoes

2 cups vegetable broth

1 teaspoon dried oregano

½ cup heavy cream

kosher salt and black pepper

Asiago tortilla crisps (see page 62)

1. In a large saucepan, melt the butter over medium heat. Add the onion, celery, carrots, and bell pepper. Cook, stirring occasionally, until the vegetables are softened, 8 to 10 minutes. Add the garlic and cook, stirring constantly, for 30 seconds.

2. Stir in the tomatoes, vegetable broth, and oregano. Bring to a simmer and then reduce heat to low and simmer, uncovered, until the vegetables are very soft and the tomatoes are falling apart, 20 to 25 minutes. Remove from the heat. Allow to cool slightly, then transfer to a blender and puree until smooth, making sure to crack open the lid a little to let steam escape. Return the soup to the pot, stir in the cream, and season to taste with salt and pepper.

3. To serve, spoon soup into individual bowls. Float one or two Asiago tortilla crisps on top of the soup and pass the rest for dipping.

● ● ● ● ● ● ● ●

ASIAGO TORTILLA CRISPS

3 small (6-inch) flour tortillas
¼ cup finely grated Asiago cheese (1 ounce)

Preheat the oven to 350°F. Cut the tortillas into 8 wedges each. Spread in a single layer on a rimmed baking sheet. Prick all over with a fork. Bake until crisp, 10 to 12 minutes, turning over halfway through cooking. Sprinkle lightly with the cheese, turn on the oven's broiler, and broil until the cheese is melted and bubbly, 2 to 3 minutes. Let cool before serving.

WHITE CHILI WITH GREEN CHILES AND CHICKEN

This dish is a nice alternative to traditional chili made with kidney beans and tomatoes. The tortillas are actually a "secret ingredient" in this thick stew; they're blended into the broth to act as a thickener, as well as to add their distinctive ground-corn flavor. The amount of chiles you add to this depends on how spicy the chiles are to begin with. Canned chiles are typically milder than fresh or frozen New Mexico Hatch chiles. **Serves 6 to 8**

1 tablespoon vegetable oil

2 small yellow onions, diced

2 cloves garlic, minced

6 cups chicken broth

2 cups dried navy beans, soaked overnight

¼ to ½ cups chopped green chiles

1 tablespoon cumin

1 teaspoon oregano

1 pound boneless, skinless chicken thighs, cut into 1-inch cubes

3 small (6-inch) corn tortillas

kosher salt and black pepper

Toppings: chopped fresh cilantro, shredded cheese, diced avocado, chopped scallions, and sour cream

1. Heat the oil in a large Dutch oven or heavy soup pot over medium heat. Add the onions and cook, stirring occasionally, until softened, 5 to 7 minutes. Add the garlic and cook, stirring constantly, for 30 seconds. Add the chicken broth, beans, chiles, cumin, oregano, and chicken. Bring to a simmer, and then reduce heat to low and simmer, partially covered, until the beans are tender and the chicken is cooked through, about 1½ hours.

2. Tear the tortillas into small pieces and place them in a medium bowl. Ladle about 1 cup of the broth out of the soup and over the tortillas. Let soak for about 5 minutes, then cook an immersion blender to puree the tortillas and broth mixture until smooth. Stir the mixture back into the soup. Season to taste with salt and pepper.

3. Serve in bowls and let each person top their chili with their favorite fixings.

• • • • • • • •

SOUTHWESTERN CAESAR SALAD

My husband's love for Caesar salads prompted me to try making a Southwestern version that would incorporate crunchy tortilla pieces instead of croutons. This recipe is a great accompaniment to any sort of Southwestern main course, like enchiladas or chili. The "croutons" are great on soups, other types of salad, or to eat like chips with dip or salsa. **Serves 4**

Smoky Tortilla "Croutons":

4 small (6-inch) flour tortillas

2 tablespoons extra-virgin olive oil

1 teaspoon smoked paprika

1 teaspoon kosher salt

Salad:

juice of 2 limes (about 4 tablespoons)

1 teaspoon Dijon mustard

1 clove garlic, minced

2 tablespoons mayonnaise

¼ cup finely grated Parmesan cheese (1 ounce)

¼ cup extra-virgin olive oil

1 head romaine lettuce

1. To make the tortilla croutons: Preheat the oven to 375°F. Brush the tortillas with olive oil on both sides. Cut the tortillas with a knife, clean kitchen shears, or a pizza wheel into strips about 1 x 2 inches. Place them in a bowl and sprinkle lightly with the paprika and salt, using your hands or a spatula to toss the tortillas to evenly coat. Spread in a single layer on a rimmed baking sheet and bake until crisp, 10 to 12 minutes. Let cool completely on the baking sheet before serving.

2. To make the salad: In a small bowl, whisk together the lime juice, mustard, garlic, mayonnaise, and Parmesan cheese until smooth. While whisking, drizzle in the olive oil until the dressing is smooth and emulsified. Just before serving, tear the lettuce by hand into bite-size pieces and place in a serving bowl. Drizzle with the dressing and toss to coat. Top with the tortilla croutons.

• • • • • • • • •

THE ULTIMATE MEXICAN SALAD

Use this recipe as a starting point for what you'd define as the "ultimate" Mexican salad. Anything goes—grilled chicken or steak, sautéed shrimp, your favorite veggies, or chopped nuts. This salad is substantial enough to be dinner on its own, a great option for a hot summer day. **Serves 4**

Tortilla Bowls:

4 large (10 to 12-inch) flour tortillas

1 tablespoon vegetable oil

kosher salt

Dressing:

juice of 1 lime (about 2 tablespoons)

1 teaspoon Dijon mustard

1 teaspoon agave syrup or honey

¼ teaspoon ground cumin

⅛ teaspoon kosher salt, or as needed

pinch cayenne pepper

¼ cup extra-virgin olive oil

Salad:

1 large head green leaf or romaine lettuce

1 (15-ounce) can black beans, drained and rinsed

1 cup frozen roasted corn, thawed

1 large globe tomato, diced

1 medium jicama, peeled and diced

¼ cup pickled jalapeños

1 medium avocado, diced

¼ cup toasted pepitas (pumpkin seeds) or shelled, roasted sunflower seeds

1 cup shredded pepper Jack cheese (4 ounces)

1. To make the tortilla bowls: Preheat the oven to 375°F. Brush the tortillas with vegetable oil on both sides and sprinkle lightly with salt. Drape a tortilla over an inverted flat-bottomed ovenproof metal mixing bowl, gently folding to form to the sides and pressing it against the bottom of the bowl so that the tortilla "bowl" will have a flat base. Repeat to make 4 tortilla bowls. Working in batches if you don't have enough bowls, bake the tortillas on the inverted bowls until the tortillas are crisp and hold their shape, 10 to 15 minutes. Let cool completely before filling.

2. To make the dressing: In a small bowl, whisk together the lime juice, mustard, agave syrup or honey, cumin, salt, and cayenne pepper. While whisking, gradually drizzle in the olive oil until the dressing is smooth and emulsified. Season with additional salt to taste, if needed. Before serving, whisk the dressing again to re-emulsify the ingredients.

3. To make the salad: Divide the lettuce among the 4 tortilla bowls, filling each bowl about two-thirds full. Layer on the remaining ingredients: black beans, corn, tomato, jicama, jalapeños, avocado, pepitas, and cheese. Drizzle with the dressing. Serve immediately.

• • • • • • • • •

GREEN CHILE CREAMED CORN WITH BLUE CORN CHIP TOPPING

A worthy side dish to accompany grilled steaks, fish tacos, or roasted chicken, this creamed corn gets some spice and color thanks to a can of green chiles and a generous sprinkling of blue corn tortilla chips, which are available in the snack aisle of most natural food stores or well-stocked supermarkets. **Serves 4**

1 tablespoon unsalted butter

1 small onion, finely diced

1 (16-ounce) bag frozen corn

2 tablespoons diced roasted green chiles, fresh, frozen or canned

kosher salt and black pepper

2 cups blue corn tortilla chips, crushed (about 2¼ ounces)

1. In a large skillet, melt the butter over medium heat. Add the onions and cook, stirring occasionally, until translucent, 5 to 7 minutes. Add the frozen corn and green chiles and cook, stirring occasionally, until the corn thaws and begins to soften, about 5 minutes. Add the cream, reduce the heat to low, and simmer, uncovered, until the cream has reduced and thickened slightly, about 10 minutes. Season to taste with salt and pepper. Transfer to a serving bowl and sprinkle with the crushed tortilla chips.

• • • • • • • • •

CRUNCHY CILANTRO SLAW

Take this addictive slaw to a potluck. It's on the spicy side, thanks to the pickled jalapeños, but it's a great dish to go with burgers, barbecue, mac-and-cheese, and other crowd-friendly fare. If you'll be serving a lot of kids or people who don't tolerate spicy food well, you can omit the jalapeños (or replace them with canned green chiles, which are milder).

Serves 8

Tortilla Crisps:

3 small (6-inch) corn tortillas

vegetable oil spray

1 teaspoon taco seasoning

Dressing:

1 teaspoon Dijon mustard

3 tablespoons cider vinegar

⅛ teaspoon kosher salt

2 tablespoons extra-virgin olive oil

Slaw:

10 ounces shredded cabbage (about 2½ cups)

2 medium carrots, peeled and shredded

¼ cup chopped pickled jalapeños

¼ cup chopped fresh cilantro

1. To make the tortilla crisps: Preheat the oven to 375°F. Using a knife, clean kitchen shears, or a pizza wheel, cut the tortillas in half and then crosswise into ½-inch strips. Place the tortilla strips in a bowl and spray or drizzle with vegetable oil just to coat, then sprinkle with the taco seasoning. Spread in an even layer on a rimmed baking sheet and bake until crisp, about 15 minutes. Let cool completely on the baking sheet.

2. To make the dressing: In a small bowl, whisk together the mustard, vinegar, and salt. While whisking, drizzle in the olive oil until the dressing is smooth and emulsified.

3. To make the slaw: In a serving bowl, toss together the cabbage, carrots, jalapeños or green chiles, and cilantro until well-combined. Drizzle with the dressing, cover, and refrigerate for 30 minutes or up to several hours, or until the cabbage mixture is slightly wilted. Just before serving, toss with the tortilla strips to redistribute the dressing and mix in the tortillas.

· · · · · · · · ·

WRAPS *and* 'RITOS

By their very nature, tortillas are designed to be wrapped around
a tasty filling. What filling that may be can range wildly as
inspiration hits. From a wide variety of burritos to various wrap
sandwiches, these recipes are all about the many ways you can
fill up your tortilla.

CALEXICO BURRITO

This traditional burrito is my attempt to re-create my usual order at La Taqueria, a now-defunct Tex-Mex restaurant I frequented when I lived in Brooklyn, New York. El Taq, as we called it, had a psychedelic surfer vibe, Grateful Dead on the stereo, and barely scraped by its health inspections, but it never failed to satisfy my hunger. **Serves 4**

1 (15-ounce) can black beans, undrained

2 cups cooked brown rice

4 medium (8-inch) flour tortillas

1 cup shredded Monterey Jack cheese (4 ounces)

1 medium avocado, peeled and sliced

1 small head green leaf lettuce, shredded

1 medium globe tomato, diced

1 (4-ounce) can sliced black olives

1 cup prepared salsa

½ cup plain Greek-style yogurt or low-fat sour cream

1. Heat the black beans in a small saucepan over medium-low heat until warmed through, stirring occasionally.

2. Divide the brown rice among the tortillas. Top each with about ½ cup beans, draining the excess liquid with a spoon. Let each person add their favorite toppings, including cheese, avocado, lettuce, tomato, black olives, salsa, and yogurt or sour cream. Wrap like a burrito (see page 75) and serve.

• • • • • • • • •

CALABACITAS BURRITO

Calabacitas is a New Mexican dish that usually consists of sautéed zucchini and corn. It's one of those recipes that can vary widely according to who's in the kitchen. I discovered that the concoction makes a great burrito filling when I had some leftovers in my fridge, but now I often make up a batch of calabacitas specifically to use in a burrito. It's a particularly good way to bulk burritos up if you don't want to include meat. **Serves 4**

1 tablespoon unsalted butter

1 medium shallot, diced

1 medium zucchini, diced

kernels from 2 ears corn or 1 cup frozen corn, thawed

1 (4-ounce) can chopped green chiles or ½ cup fresh, roasted green chiles

1 (15-ounce) can pinto beans, undrained

4 medium (8-inch) flour tortillas

1 cup shredded Monterey Jack cheese (4 ounces)

kosher salt and black pepper

1. To make the calabacitas, melt the butter over medium heat in a large nonstick skillet. Add the shallot and cook, stirring frequently, until softened and translucent, about 4 minutes. Add the zucchini and the corn and cook, stirring occasionally, until the vegetables are tender, about 7 minutes. Stir in the chiles and season to taste with salt and pepper.

2. To make the burritos, warm the beans in a small saucepan over medium heat until heated through. Warm the tortillas over an open burner for about 15 seconds on each side or in the microwave on high power for about 15 seconds. Divide the beans among the tortillas, draining the excess liquid with a slotted spoon. Divide the calabacitas among the burritos and top with the cheese. Wrap like a burrito (see sidebar) and serve immediately.

• • • • • • • • •

HOW TO WRAP A BURRITO

Perfectly rolling a burrito or wrap every time isn't hard with a few easy steps:

1. Wrap the bottom edge (closest to you) of the tortilla over the filling.

2. Fold the two opposite sides over the filling.

3. Roll the packet away from you, ending with the edge of the tortilla on the underside.

CALIFORNIA BURRITO

As I started brainstorming recipes for this book, colleagues on the West Coast insisted I include the California burrito. I'd never heard of such a thing, so I did a little research. Imagine my surprise to find that it's a burrito that includes—among other things— french fries! I re-created the burrito as best as I could, and discovered that it's a real taste sensation: salty and hearty and meaty, with the guacamole and sour cream adding freshness. If you make Carne Asada Tacos (page 108), make a little extra meat to fold into one of these burritos for another meal. **Serves 4**

1 (16-ounce) bag frozen oven-style french fries

2 medium ripe avocados

1 small globe tomato, diced

2 tablespoons minced onion

1 tablespoon chopped jalapeño

2 tablespoons chopped cilantro

juice of 1 lime (about 2 tablespoons)

4 medium (8-inch) flour tortillas

1 pound cooked carne asada (page 108)

1 cup shredded cheddar cheese (4 ounces)

½ cup sour cream

kosher salt

1. Bake the french fries in the oven according to the package directions. While the fries are cooking, make the guacamole: Scoop the flesh of the avocados into a bowl and mash with a fork until smooth and creamy. Add the tomatoes, onions, jalapeño, and cilantro, and stir to combine. Stir in the lime juice and season to taste with salt.

2. To make the burritos, warm the tortillas over an open burner for about 15 seconds on each side or stacked in the microwave on high power for about 15 seconds. Divide the carne asada among the tortillas. Top each with a handful of french fries and a sprinkling of cheese. Add a scoop of guacamole and a spoonful or two of sour cream. Wrap like a burrito (see page 75) and serve.

• • • • • • • • •

GRILLED STACKER

I actually can't take credit for the stroke of genius that is the Stacker. A cross between a burrito and a pressed, panini-type sandwich, the Stacker is on the menu at a burrito chain restaurant that my family loves to visit. Use a panini press or a contact grill (like a George Foreman grill) to make this. **Makes 2**

⅔ cup canned black beans, undrained

2 large (12-inch) flour tortillas

⅔ cup cooked brown rice

¼ cup shredded Colby or Monterey Jack cheese (2 ounces)

2 tablespoons sliced black olives

¼ cup prepared salsa or pico de gallo

½ cup tortilla chips, broken into smaller pieces (about ½ ounce)

2 tablespoons sour cream

2 tablespoons pickled jalapeños

1 tablespoon vegetable oil

1. In a small saucepan, warm the beans over medium-low heat. Stack the tortillas and microwave on high power until soft and pliable, about 15 seconds.

2. Place half of the beans in the center of each tortilla. Top each with half of the rice. Sprinkle with the cheese, black olives, and salsa. Add the tortilla chips and top with a dollop of sour cream and a few jalapeños. Wrap like burritos (see page 75). Lightly press the burritos, seam-side down, to flatten a little. Heat a panini press or a contact grill to high heat. Brush the cooking surface lightly with vegetable oil. Place the burritos on the grill and press down to flatten. Cook until the tortillas are lightly browned and a little crisp, about 5 minutes. Remove from grill and serve immediately.

• • • • • • • •

CHILI DOG WRAPS

A batch of chili goes a long way if you wrap it up in a tortilla with a hot dog. This is a great way to make use of leftover chili, or you can use this recipe to whip up a batch for the express purpose of making these chili dogs. **Serves 6**

1 tablespoon vegetable oil

1 medium yellow onion, diced

1 small green bell pepper, diced

2 cloves garlic, minced

1 (15-ounce) can black beans, drained and rinsed

1 (15-ounce) can kidney beans, drained and rinsed

1 (28-ounce can) crushed tomatoes

2 tablespoons tomato paste

1 tablespoon ground cumin

2 to 3 teaspoons red chile powder

½ teaspoon chipotle powder

¼ teaspoon kosher salt

6 hot dogs

6 medium (8-inch) flour tortillas

1½ cups shredded Colby cheese (6 ounces)

1. In large saucepan or Dutch oven, heat the vegetable oil over medium-high heat. Add the onion and pepper and cook, stirring occasionally, until soft, about 7 minutes. Add the garlic and cook, stirring constantly, for 30 seconds. Add the beans, tomatoes, and tomato paste and stir to combine. Add the cumin, chile, chipotle powder, and salt. Bring to a simmer, reduce the heat to low and cook for 15 to 20 minutes, allowing the flavors to meld. Add the hot dogs and simmer until the hot dogs are heated through, about 10 minutes.

2. Warm the tortillas over an open burner for about 15 seconds on each side, or stack and microwave on high power for 15 seconds. Using a pair of tongs, remove the hot dogs from the chili and place one dog in the center of each tortilla. Spoon some chili over the dogs and sprinkle with cheese. Wrap like a burrito (see page 78) and serve immediately.

· · · · · · · · ·

BBQ AND SLAW WRAP

Making pulled chicken is easy as can be in a slow cooker, and if you use your favorite store-bought barbecue sauce, it only requires three ingredients. Let the chicken simmer all day, and then whip up the slaw just before serving. **Serves 6**

Pulled Chicken:

3 pounds boneless, skinless chicken breasts and thighs

1 large yellow onion, diced

1½ cups prepared barbecue sauce

Slaw:

¼ cup mayonnaise

1 tablespoon white vinegar

¼ teaspoon kosher salt

⅛ teaspoon black pepper

¼ teaspoon hot sauce, such as Texas Pete or Tabasco

1 (6-ounce) package shredded cabbage (about 1½ cups)

6 medium (8-inch) flour tortillas

1. To make the chicken: Place the chicken in a medium or large slow cooker. Sprinkle with the onions and pour the sauce over the top, using a spoon to spread it to completely coat the chicken. Cover the slow cooker and cook on low until the chicken's internal temperature registers at least 165°F when checked with a meat thermometer, 5 to 6 hours. Remove the chicken pieces from the cooker and let cool for a few minutes, then use forks, a knife, or your clean hands to chop or pull the chicken into small shreds. Return the shredded chicken to the slow cooker and stir it into the sauce.

2. To make the slaw: In a large bowl, whisk together the mayonnaise, vinegar, salt, pepper, and hot sauce until smooth. Add the cabbage and use salad servers or tongs to toss until evenly coated. Refrigerate until ready to serve.

3. Warm the tortillas over an open burner for about 15 seconds on each side or stack and microwave on high power for 15 seconds. Place some pulled chicken in the center of a tortilla and top with slaw. Wrap like a burrito (see page 75). Repeat with the remaining tortillas and filling. Serve immediately.

· · · · · · · ·

BLTA TACOS

The BLT is hands-down my favorite sandwich, and if it has A in it— that's short for avocado—so much the better! I find a BLT in wrap form easier to eat than one on toast because you don't risk losing stray pieces of bacon or tomato. **Serves 4**

12 slices thick-cut bacon

6 ounces plain Greek-style yogurt

1 tablespoon mayonnaise

1 tablespoon chopped green chiles

1 tablespoon chopped fresh cilantro

8 small (6-inch) flour tortillas

1 large tomato, diced

1 small head green leaf lettuce, chopped

1 medium ripe avocado, peeled, pitted, and sliced

1. Line a plate with paper towels. Working in batches if necessary, place the bacon in a large skillet over medium heat. Cook until crisp, turning over to cook evenly, about 7 to 9 minutes total. Transfer the bacon to the prepared plate.

2. While the bacon is cooking, in a small bowl, stir together the yogurt, mayonnaise, green chiles, and cilantro.

3. Warm the tortillas over an open burner for about 15 seconds on each side or stack and microwave on high power for 15 seconds. To assemble the wraps, break the bacon in half and put three pieces in a tortilla. Add some tomatoes, lettuce, and avocado. Drizzle with a tablespoon or two of the yogurt sauce. Fold the sides of the tortillas over the filling, taco-style. Serve immediately.

• • • • • • • • •

CEVICHE ROLL-UPS

Ceviche, in which fish is "cooked" in acidic liquid like lime and lemon juice, seems like an exotic, complicated recipe, but really it's not that hard to make at home. The key is to begin with the freshest fish you can find, from a reputable fishmonger. Firm white fish such as flounder, grouper, bass, or sole is best in this recipe. **Serves 4**

1 pound firm white fish, diced into ¼-inch pieces

2 tablespoons minced red onion

2 teaspoons minced jalapeño

1 teaspoon kosher salt

juice of 2 limes plus juice of 1 lemon (to make ½ cup citrus juice)

4 large leaves romaine lettuce

4 medium (8-inch) flour tortillas

1 medium avocado, peeled and sliced

¼ cup chopped fresh cilantro leaves

1. Spread the fish in a glass baking dish. Sprinkle with the onion, jalapeño, and salt. Pour the citrus juice over the fish and stir to combine. Cover with plastic wrap and refrigerate for 15 to 20 minutes, turning over the mixture with a spoon every 5 minutes to ensure that the fish comes into even contact with the citrus juice. The fish is ready when it's opaque.

2. To serve, place a lettuce leaf in the middle of a tortilla. Spoon some of the ceviche onto the leaf and top with a few slices of avocado and a sprinkling of cilantro. Wrap like a burrito (see page 75). Repeat with the remaining tortillas. Cut in half on the diagonal and serve immediately.

• • • • • • • •

SHRIMP PO' BOY WRAPS

Frozen breaded shrimp, baked in the oven, are a handy stand-in for the typically deep-fried shrimp in this riff on a New Orleans favorite. A rémoulade sauce is easy to whip up with ingredients you're likely to have on hand in your fridge or pantry. You could also make this wrap with grilled shrimp, fried oysters, or frozen fish sticks.

Serves 4

1 pound large breaded, frozen tail-off shrimp

½ cup mayonnaise

1 tablespoon ketchup

2 teaspoons Dijon mustard

1 teaspoon freshly squeezed lemon juice

1 teaspoon Worcestershire sauce

1 scallion, minced

1 small rib celery, minced

¼ teaspoon garlic powder

½ teaspoon paprika

4 medium (8-inch) flour tortillas

1 small head green leaf lettuce, shredded

1 large globe tomato, diced

1. Cook the shrimp in the oven according to package directions.

2. While the shrimp is cooking, make the rémoulade sauce: In a bowl, combine the mayonnaise, ketchup, mustard, lemon juice, Worcestershire sauce, scallion, celery, garlic powder, and paprika. Stir with a spoon until smooth. Refrigerate, covered, until needed.

3. Warm the tortillas over an open burner until warm and pliable, about 15 seconds per side, or stack and microwave on high power for 20 seconds. Divide the shrimp among the tortillas. Top with lettuce and tomato, and drizzle with the rémoulade sauce. Wrap like a burrito (see page 75) and serve immediately.

· · · · · · · · ·

MEDITERRANEAN HUMMUS WRAP

This fresh-tasting wrap is sturdy enough to pack for a lunch. It's a healthy and interesting alternative to the usual sandwich. With all the various hummus flavors available in most stores, you can get creative with this wrap. My favorite is roasted red pepper hummus, but there is also hummus flavored with kalamata olives, hot peppers, sun-dried tomatoes, and a variety of other ingredients. **Makes 2 sandwiches**

½ cup prepared hummus

2 medium (8-inch) flour tortillas

1 small cucumber, peeled and sliced

4 ounces alfalfa or radish sprouts

2 medium Roma tomatoes, sliced

½ cup jarred roasted red peppers, cut into strips

1 cup pitted kalamata olives (about 4 ounces), coarsely chopped or sliced

1. To make wraps, spread half of the hummus on each tortilla, leaving a border of about 1 inch uncovered. Arrange the cucumber, sprouts, tomato, red peppers, and olives in the center of each tortilla. Wrap like a burrito (see page 75). To pack in a lunch, wrap tightly in plastic wrap or aluminum foil and keep refrigerated or in an insulated container with an ice pack.

● ● ● ● ● ● ● ●

MEAT MAIN COURSES

Whether used in traditional ways, such as in fajitas or tacos, or in more unusual applications, like to crust fish or as a binder for croquettes, corn and flour tortillas are must-have ingredients for a variety of meaty entrees.

TORTILLA-CRUSTED STUFFED CHICKEN BREASTS

Chicken is much more interesting and flavorful when it's stuffed with a creamy filling and rolled in crunchy tortilla chips. I really like the way blue tortilla chips look for this recipe. They're usually available in the gourmet snack aisle, but if you have trouble finding blue chips, you could also use traditional white or yellow corn chips. If you don't have an ovenproof skillet, transfer the browned chicken breasts to a baking sheet before putting them in the oven. **Serves 4**

4 ounces cream cheese, softened

¼ cup chopped black olives

1 tablespoon prepared salsa

2 teaspoons chopped scallions, green parts only

4 cups blue corn tortilla chips (about 4½ ounces)

4 (4 to 6-ounce) boneless, skinless chicken breasts

1 tablespoon vegetable oil

1. Preheat the oven to 400°F. In a small bowl, stir together the cream cheese, black olives, salsa, and scallions. Set aside.

2. Place the tortilla chips in a large zip-top bag and use a meat mallet, a rolling pin, or the bottom of a small pan to crush the chips until they resemble coarse crumbs.

3. Cut a small slit, about 1½ inches wide, into the side of each chicken breast, moving the tip of the knife along the inside of the chicken to create a pocket for the filling. Using a small spatula or butter knife and your clean fingers, stuff about 2 tablespoons of the cream cheese filling into each breast, scraping any excess filling off the exterior of the chicken. Place a chicken breast in the zip-top bag with the tortilla chip crumbs, pressing handfuls of crumbs onto the chicken on all sides to coat. Remove the chicken breast and place on a plate, and bread the remaining breasts.

4. In a large ovenproof skillet, heat the vegetable oil over medium-high heat, then place the chicken breasts in the pan. Cook until browned, about 3 minutes on each side. Transfer the pan to the oven and cook for 20 minutes, or until the chicken's internal temperature registers at least 165°F when checked with a meat thermometer. Serve hot.

· · · · · · · · ·

CHICKEN AND BELL PEPPER FAJITAS

Make this dish on the grill, with a countertop grill, or on the stove. However you prepare them, the toppings are what really make this dish, so have on hand plenty of fresh cilantro, avocado wedges or guacamole, salsa, and anything else you might like to top your fajita. If steak's more your thing, use an equal amount of flank steak or skirt steak and cook for about 10 minutes or until the steak is cooked through.

If you're making this dish in a grill pan or skillet, you can cut the raw chicken into strips before seasoning and cooking, which will allow it to cook faster. Sauté the peppers and onions with the oil over medium-high heat for about 8 minutes. Remove the vegetables to a serving platter and keep warm under aluminum foil. Add the chicken to the pan and sauté until the chicken is cooked through, 7 to 9 minutes.

Serves 4 (makes 8 fajitas)

½ teaspoon kosher salt

½ teaspoon ground cumin

¼ teaspoon garlic powder

¼ teaspoon smoked paprika

1 cup sour cream

2 chipotle peppers in adobo sauce, coarsely chopped

1 tablespoon freshly squeezed lime juice

1 large red onion, sliced

2 medium red bell peppers, sliced into strips

1 teaspoon vegetable oil

1½ pounds boneless, skinless chicken, breasts or thighs

8 small (6-inch) flour tortillas

Toppings: avocado slices, guacamole, salsa, pico de gallo, fresh cilantro, chopped tomatoes, black olives

1. Heat a grill to medium-high heat. In a small bowl, stir together the salt, cumin, garlic powder, and paprika. Set aside. Make the chipotle sauce by placing the sour cream, chipotles, and lime juice in a bowl and pureeing with an immersion blender. Cover and refrigerate until needed.

2. Prick a piece of aluminum foil several times with a fork or the tip of a knife. Place the onion and peppers in the middle of the foil and drizzle them with the vegetable oil. Bring the sides of the foil over the vegetables and crimp it gently to seal. Place the packet on the grill.

3. Sprinkle the chicken on all sides with the spice mixture. Place it on the grill and grill, covered, until grill marks are visible, 6 to 8 minutes. Turn the chicken over with tongs and grill for an additional 6 to 8 minutes or until the chicken is cooked through and registers at least 165°F when checked with a meat thermometer. Let the chicken rest for 5 minutes, then thinly slice into strips, using tongs or a fork to hold the chicken so you don't burn your fingers.

4. Check the peppers and onions and remove from grill if they are soft and tender, or cook 5 to 8 minutes longer. Meanwhile, wrap the tortillas loosely in aluminum foil and place on the grill until warm, about 5 minutes.

5. To serve, place the chicken, peppers, and onions on a platter. Set out the toppings and the creamy chipotle sauce, and let each person assemble their own fajita.

· · · · · · · ·

GRILLED FISH TACOS

Fresh, light, and easy to prepared, grilled fish tacos are among my favorite tortilla-based meals. This recipe dresses the tacos with a simple cabbage slaw and some sliced radishes (if you have a mandoline slicer, use it to get superthin, even slices). You can use any type of fish; flaky white fish is the most traditional option. Inexpensive and commonly available tilapia is one great option, as is cod, catfish, or bass. **Serves 4 (makes 8 tacos)**

4 cups shredded napa cabbage (about 8 ounces)

1 tablespoon diced pickled jalapeño

¼ teaspoon kosher salt

2 tablespoons chopped fresh cilantro

juice of ½ lime (about 1 tablespoon)

¼ cup cornmeal

½ teaspoon ground cumin

½ teaspoon red chile powder

¼ teaspoon kosher salt

4 white fish fillets (about 1 pound total), skin and pin bones removed

vegetable oil, as needed

8 small (6-inch) corn tortillas

8 radishes, thinly sliced

1. To make the slaw, place the cabbage in a large bowl. Add the jalapeño, salt, and cilantro. Drizzle with the lime juice and toss with tongs or salad servers to mix all the ingredients together. Cover and refrigerate until needed.

2. In a shallow bowl, combine the cornmeal, cumin, red chile powder, and salt. Brush a grill pan or an outdoor grill with the vegetable oil and heat over medium-high heat. Dredge the fish in the cornmeal mixture, then place on the grill. Cook until the fish flakes easily when tested with a fork, 4 to 5 minutes. Place the fillets on a platter and break into large chunks.

3. To assemble the tacos, warm the tortillas in a dry skillet, a few seconds on each side, or stack them and microwave on high power for 20 seconds. Place a few pieces of fish in each tortilla, along with some of the cabbage slaw and a few radish slices. Serve immediately.

. . . .

TORTILLA AND PEPITA–CRUSTED FISH

This breaded fish has a crisp and flavorful crust thanks to crushed tortilla chips and roasted pepitas (pumpkin seeds). You can find pepitas in the dried fruit and nuts section of a gourmet food store or natural foods store, or sometimes in well-stocked Mexican food sections. If you can't find them, use shelled sunflower seeds instead. Tilapia and catfish both work well in this dish. **Serves 4**

4 cups tortilla chips (about 3 ounces)

½ cup roasted pepitas (pumpkin seeds)

½ teaspoon ground cumin

½ teaspoon red chile powder

¼ teaspoon kosher salt

4 (6-ounce) white fish fillets

1. Preheat the oven to 375°F. Line a rimmed baking sheet with parchment paper. Place the tortilla chips in a large zip-top bag, close the bag, and crush the chips with your hands or a small saucepan, until the chips are broken into small pieces. Add the pepitas, cumin, chile powder, and salt, and shake to combine.

2. Place the fish on the prepared baking sheet. Sprinkle a handful of the tortilla chip mixture on top of each fillet, pressing lightly to help the coating adhere. Bake the fillets until they're cooked through and the fish flakes when tested with a fork, 10 to 12 minutes. Serve hot.

• • • • • • • • •

MEXICAN CROQUETTES WITH SPICY DIPPING SAUCE

Use ground-up tortillas in place of bread crumbs in these easy croquettes. They give a denser texture and an intriguing, complex flavor.

Serves 4

3 small (6-inch) corn tortillas

12 ounces canned salmon, drained

½ cup minced red bell pepper

½ cup frozen corn, thawed

4 tablespoons mayonnaise, divided

1 tablespoon all-purpose flour

1 large egg, lightly beaten

1 tablespoon chopped fresh cilantro

¼ teaspoon kosher salt

⅛ teaspoon black pepper

2 teaspoons grated lime zest, divided

¼ cup sour cream

2 tablespoons minced pickled jalapeños

2 tablespoons vegetable oil

1. Rip the tortillas into pieces and place them in the bowl of a food processor. Pulse until the tortillas are ground into crumbs. Place 4 tablespoons of the ground tortillas in a large bowl and reserve the rest.

2. To the bowl, add the salmon, bell pepper, corn, 2 tablespoons of the mayonnaise, flour, egg, cilantro, salt, pepper, and 1 teaspoon of the lime zest. Use a spoon or your clean hands to mix well. Form into 4 patties, compressing the mixture to help it hold together. Place the patties on a plate, cover loosely with plastic wrap, and refrigerate for 30 minutes to 1 hour to help them set.

3. While the patties are chilling, make the dipping sauce: In a small bowl, stir together the sour cream, the remaining 2 tablespoons mayonnaise, the pickled jalapeños, and the remaining 1 teaspoon lime zest. Cover and refrigerate until needed.

4. Place the remaining ground tortilla in a shallow bowl or plate. Dredge the cold patties in the ground tortillas. Heat the vegetable oil in a large nonstick skillet over medium-high heat. When the oil shimmers, add the patties. Cook until the patties are crisp and have a golden crust, about 9 minutes on each side. Serve hot, with a dollop of dipping sauce.

● ● ● ● ● ● ● ●

GRILLED SALMON TOSTADAS WITH AVOCADO SAUCE

At once creamy and coolly refreshing, this dish is a great one to serve in the summer, especially if you can cook the salmon on an outdoor grill. It makes a great presentation, so it's ideal for company. **Serves 4**

1 medium ripe avocado

¼ cup sour cream

juice of 1 lime, divided (about 2 tablespoons)

½ teaspoon garlic powder

¼ teaspoon kosher salt, plus more as needed

3 tablespoons chopped fresh cilantro, divided

3 tablespoons milk

2 medium cucumbers, peeled, seeded and diced

vegetable oil, as needed

4 (5 to 6-ounce) salmon fillets

4 small (6-inch) corn tortillas

black pepper

1. Cut the avocado in half, remove the pit, and scoop the flesh into a medium bowl. Add the sour cream, half the lime juice, garlic powder, salt, and 2 tablespoons of the cilantro. Use an immersion blender to puree the ingredients until smooth. Stir in the milk, adding just enough for the sauce to be thick but pourable. Cover and refrigerate until needed.

2. In a small bowl, combine the cucumbers, the remaining half of the lime juice, and the remaining 1 tablespoon cilantro. Cover and refrigerate until needed.

3. Brush a grill pan or the grate of an outdoor grill with the vegetable oil and heat to medium-high. Season the salmon fillets with salt and pepper, and grill until grill marks appear and the outside of the fish is opaque, 4 to 5 minutes on each side. Remove from the grill and cover loosely with aluminum foil to keep warm.

4. Line a plate with paper towels. Heat about ½ inch of vegetable oil in a small skillet. One at a time, fry the tortillas in the oil until crisp, about 30 seconds on each side. Drain for a moment on the paper towels to blot excess oil.

5. To serve, place a tortilla on a plate and top with a spoonful of the cucumber salad. Place a salmon fillet on the cucumbers and drizzle the avocado sauce over the dish.

· · · · · · · · ·

TEQUILA SHRIMP TACOS

A *splash of tequila brightens these sautéed shrimp. But don't worry; the alcohol burns off during cooking, so they're even appropriate for kids to eat. Serve these tacos alongside rice and beans, or make the shrimp on their own to top a taco salad.* **Serves 4**

2 tablespoons white tequila

juice of 1 lime (about 2 tablespoons)

1 tablespoon vegetable oil

1 pound medium shrimp, peeled and deveined

2 tablespoons chopped fresh cilantro

8 small (6-inch) corn tortillas

1 medium head iceberg lettuce, shredded

1 medium avocado, sliced

4 radishes, thinly sliced

1 cup prepared salsa or pico de gallo sauce (8 ounces)

kosher salt and black pepper

1. In a small bowl, combine the tequila and lime juice. Heat the vegetable oil in a large skillet over medium-high heat. Add the shrimp and cook, stirring frequently, just until the shrimp turn pink and opaque, about 3 minutes.

2. Pour the tequila-lime mixture into the pan, increase the heat to high, and toss the shrimp in the liquid until the liquid comes to a boil and reduces by roughly half. Sprinkle the cilantro over the shrimp and season to taste with salt and pepper.

3. To serve, warm the tortillas in a dry skillet for 10 seconds on each side or stack and microwave on high power for 20 seconds. Place 3 to 4 shrimp in a tortilla, top with lettuce, avocado, and radish, drizzle with salsa or pico de gallo, and fold the tortillas over the filling, taco-style. Serve hot or warm.

• • • • • • • • •

BURGER POUCHES

A seasoned beef patty is tucked into a tortilla with all the usual toppings, then pressed on a grill. The result: a gooey, juicy, delicious mess of a meal! Use a contact grill, such as a George Foreman, or a panini press to make these addictive burger creations. **Serves 4**

1 pound ground beef

½ teaspoon Worcestershire sauce

¼ teaspoon garlic powder

¼ teaspoon kosher salt

⅛ teaspoon black pepper

4 large (10 to 12-inch) flour tortillas

4 slices American or Colby cheese

4 slices globe tomato

4 leaves iceberg or romaine lettuce

1. Place the beef in a bowl and use clean hands to mix the Worcestershire sauce, garlic powder, salt, and pepper into the beef. Form the beef into 4 patties about ½ inch thick.

2. Heat a grill or a grill pan over medium-high heat. Grill the burgers until cooked through but still barely pink on the inside, 6 to 8 minutes, turning once.

3. Place a piece of cheese in the middle of each tortilla. Place the burger on the cheese, then the tomato and lettuce over the burger. Beginning with one side of the tortilla, fold the edges of the tortilla gradually over the burger, overlapping the edge of the previous fold to cover the filling completely. Heat a contact grill or panini grill over high heat. Place the burger pouches on the grill, folded-side down, and press the top grill lightly over the pouches. Cook until the tortilla is toasted, about 5 minutes. Serve immediately.

• • • • • • • •

ROPA VIEJA TACOS

A slow cooker is the best way to cook the steak for these tacos—the long, low simmer will help the flavors develop and result in meat that's falling-apart tender. If you don't have a slow cooker, though, use a large, heavy pot, such as a Dutch oven, and cook it on the stovetop on low for 1½ to 2 hours, until the meat is tender enough to be shredded with a fork. **Serves 6 (makes 12 tacos)**

2 pounds flank steak, trimmed of excess fat

1 small red onion, sliced

1 medium red bell pepper, cut into strips

1 medium green bell pepper, cut into strips

1 (14.5-ounce) can diced tomatoes

1 cup vegetable or beef broth

2 teaspoons ground cumin

1 teaspoon dried Mexican oregano (or traditional oregano)

juice of 1 lime (about 2 tablespoons)

1½ teaspoons extra-virgin olive oil

1 (8-ounce) package chopped salad greens, such as romaine or green leaf lettuce

12 small (6-inch) flour tortillas

kosher salt and black pepper

1. Cut the steak into several large pieces to fit into the crock of your slow cooker. Season the steak on both sides with salt and pepper. Heat a large skillet over medium-high heat and brown the steak on all sides, about 2 to 3 minutes per side.

2. Place half of the onion and the red and green bell peppers in the bottom of the slow cooker. Place the steak on top of the vegetables, then place the rest of the onion and peppers on top of the steak. In a bowl, combine the tomatoes, vegetable or beef broth, cumin, and oregano. Pour the mixture over the vegetables and steak in the crock. Cook until the meat is soft enough to pull apart easily with a fork, 4 to 5 hours on high or 8 to 10 hours on low. Working with two forks, pull the meat into shreds and keep warm in the slow cooker on the "keep warm" setting until ready to serve.

3. Just before serving, in a small bowl, whisk together the lime juice, a pinch of salt, and the olive oil. Place the salad greens in a medium bowl and pour the lime mixture over the leaves, tossing with tongs or salad servers to coat evenly.

4. Warm the tortillas over an open burner for about 15 seconds on each side or stacked in the microwave on high power for 15 seconds. To serve, use tongs or a slotted spoon to scoop up some meat, holding it over the crock for a moment to let most of the liquid drain off. Place the meat inside a tortilla, top with some lettuce, and fold the tortilla over the filling, taco-style.

● ● ● ● ● ● ● ●

FLANK STEAK AND CARAMELIZED ONION ENCHILADAS

Caramelized onions add a surprising, sweet element to rolled enchiladas. Use prepared enchilada sauce (I like the Buena Comida brand) or make your own. **Serves 4 (makes 8 enchiladas)**

2 tablespoons vegetable oil, divided, plus more for frying

2 large sweet or yellow onions, halved and sliced

1½ pounds flank steak

8 small (6-inch) corn tortillas

1½ cups shredded Monterey Jack cheese (6 ounces), divided

1 (15-ounce) can enchilada sauce

kosher salt and black pepper

1. Heat 1 tablespoon of the vegetable oil in a large skillet over medium-low heat. Add the onions and cook, stirring occasionally, until very soft and dark golden brown, about 15 minutes. Transfer the onions to a heatproof tray and cover loosely with aluminum foil to keep warm.

2. In the same pan, heat the remaining 1 tablespoon vegetable oil over medium-high heat. Season the steak with salt and pepper and place in the hot pan. Cook until the steak is browned but still pink in the middle, about 5 minutes on each side. The steak should reach an internal temperature of 145°F when checked with a meat thermometer. Let cool slightly, then cut into thin strips, slicing against the grain of the meat.

3. Preheat the oven to 350°F. Warm the tortillas in a dry skillet until pliable, or stack and microwave on high power for 20 seconds. Place a few strips of steak and a little onion in a tortilla, plus a bit of cheese, reserving about ½ cup of cheese to sprinkle on top. Roll the tortillas around the filling and place in a 9 x 13-inch glass baking dish. Repeat with the remaining ingredients. Pour the enchilada sauce over the rolled enchiladas and sprinkle with the remaining ½ cup cheese. Bake until heated through and the cheese is melted, 20 to 25 minutes. Serve hot.

· · · · · · · · ·

CARNE ASADA TACOS

Roughly translating as "grilled meat," carne asada is a tasty, easy-to-prepare filling for tacos and burritos. The marinade gives the meat extra zing. The most delicious—and traditional—way to cook the meat is over an open flame, but if you don't have an outdoor grill, use a countertop grill or a grill pan as hot as you can make it so that you get some good grill marks. **Serves 4**

juice of 2 limes (about ¼ cup)

1 tablespoon Worcestershire sauce

½ teaspoon kosher salt

⅛ teaspoon black pepper

1 tablespoon extra-virgin olive oil

2 pounds flank steak or skirt steak, trimmed of excess fat

vegetable oil, as needed

8 small (6-inch) corn tortillas

1 medium red onion, thinly sliced

1 small bunch fresh cilantro

1 medium avocado, sliced

1. In a large zip-top bag, combine the lime juice, Worcestershire sauce, salt, pepper, and olive oil. Add the steak and seal the bag, pressing out excess air. Work the steak around in the bag, making sure it's coated completely with the marinade. Refrigerate for 30 minutes to 1 hour.

2. Heat an outdoor grill, a countertop grill, or a grill pan to high heat. Brush the grilling surface with the vegetable oil. Cook the meat until grill marks appear, about 5 minutes on each side. Let rest on a cutting board for 5 minutes, then thinly slice the meat against the grain and arrange on a platter.

3. Heat the tortillas in a dry skillet for about 15 seconds on each side, or stack and microwave on high power for 20 seconds. Keep the tortillas warm in a tortilla warmer or folded inside a clean dishtowel. Set out the red onion, cilantro, and avocado, and let each person make their own tacos with the meat and toppings.

• • • • • • • • •

PHILLY CHEESE STEAK TACOS

There's a restaurant in my neighborhood that has a taco menu with all sorts of crazy concoctions (including an off-the-menu BLT taco that inspired my BLTA Tacos on page 83). From gyros to Cobb salad to Buffalo chicken, their tacos are far from authentic Mexican fare, but they're really fun and amazingly addictive! My favorite is their riff on the Philly cheese steak, which prompted me to try creating my own version at home. Using roast beef from the deli and a jar of Cheez Whiz makes this a quick meal, but sliced American cheese or provolone are also classic toppings. If you prefer to use sliced cheese, assemble the tacos on a rimmed baking sheet and melt the cheese under a preheated broiler for 2 to 3 minutes. **Serves 4 (makes 8 tacos)**

1 tablespoon vegetable oil

1 medium yellow onion, thinly sliced

1 green bell pepper, halved, seeded, and thinly sliced

1 pound deli-sliced roast beef, coarsely chopped

1 (8-ounce) jar Cheez Whiz

8 small (6-inch) flour tortillas

1. Heat the vegetable oil over medium heat in a large nonstick skillet. Add the onion and bell pepper and cook, stirring frequently, until the vegetables are very soft, about 10 minutes. Transfer the vegetables to a platter or a shallow bowl and cover loosely with aluminum foil to keep warm.

2. Increase the heat to medium-high, add the roast beef to the skillet, and cook, stirring occasionally, until heated through, 3 to 4 minutes. Transfer to a platter and keep warm under aluminum foil.

3. Spoon the Cheese Whiz into a small microwave-safe bowl and heat on high power until melted, 20 to 30 seconds. Warm the tortillas over an open burner, or stack and microwave on high power for 20 seconds.

4. To assemble the tacos, place some beef on a warmed tortilla. Top with some of the onion and pepper mixture, and drizzle with about 2 tablespoons of the melted Cheese Whiz. Fold the tortillas over the filling, taco-style, and serve hot.

• • • • • • • • •

MEATLESS MAINS

Tortillas (and the Mexican/Southwestern cuisine that they're part of) can be a vegetarian's best friend. After all, you can put just about anything inside of, or on top of, a tortilla. And traditional toppings like beans, cheese, and avocado are filling and high in protein and other nutrients. Vegetarians, or home cooks who are trying to eat less meat, will love these creative ways of using tortillas to make tantalizing and satisfying main courses. Just make sure to check that the tortillas you buy don't contain lard; flour tortillas sometimes do.

WHITE BEAN AND GUACAMOLE TOSTADAS

Tostadas are a fun alternative to tacos. Because they're eaten with a knife and fork, they seem a little more substantial than their handheld counterparts. I like using white beans for an untraditional twist (most Mexican dishes use black beans or pinto beans), and their creamy mellowness is offset by the fresh, tangy flavor of the guacamole. If you're making the guacamole an hour or two in advance, you can keep it from browning by pushing the pits into the mixture and covering it with plastic wrap, pressing the wrap right against the surface of the guacamole. **Serves 6**

Guacamole:

3 medium ripe avocados

1 large globe tomato, diced

2 teaspoons diced jalapeño

juice of ½ lime (about 1 tablespoon)

1 tablespoon chopped fresh cilantro

Tostadas:

1 tablespoon vegetable oil, plus more as needed

1 large yellow onion, minced

1 (28-ounce) can white beans, drained and rinsed

2 (4-ounce) cans chopped green chiles

2 teaspoons ground cumin

12 small (6-inch) corn tortillas

1½ cups shredded Monterey Jack cheese (6 ounces)

kosher salt and black pepper

1. To make the guacamole: Halve the avocados, remove the pits, and scoop the flesh into a medium bowl. Stir in the tomato, jalapeño, lime juice, and cilantro. Season to taste with salt. Set aside.

2. To make the tostadas: In a medium saucepan, heat 1 tablespoon vegetable oil over medium heat. Add the onion and cook, stirring occasionally, until softened, 5 to 7 minutes. Add the beans, green chiles, and cumin. Cook, stirring occasionally, until the mixture is heated through, about 5 minutes. Season to taste with salt and pepper, cover to keep warm, and set aside.

3. Preheat the oven to the warm setting, about 170°F, and line a rimmed baking sheet with paper towels. Pour vegetable oil into a small skillet to a depth of about ½ inch. Heat the oil over medium heat until it shimmers. Fry each tortilla for about 1 minute, turning over halfway through cooking, until the edges begin to crisp. Remove the tortillas with tongs and drain between layers of paper towels on the prepared baking sheet and keep warm in the low oven.

4. To serve, spread guacamole on a tortilla. Top with a spoonful of beans and a sprinkle of cheese. Stack a second tortilla on top, and repeat the toppings with guacamole, beans, and cheese. Serve warm.

• • • • • • • •

BROCCOLI-CHEDDAR QUICHE

Made with a crust of ground corn tortillas, this quiche is a delicious option for a brunch or as a simple supper, paired with a green salad. If you want to use fresh broccoli, chop it into bite-size pieces and steam it in a little water until tender. **Serves 4 to 6**

10 small (6-inch) corn tortillas, torn into pieces

¼ cup all-purpose flour

½ teaspoon kosher salt, divided

1 tablespoon vegetable oil

¼ cup warm water

5 large eggs

⅓ cup heavy cream

½ cup milk

⅛ teaspoon black pepper

1 cup chopped frozen broccoli, thawed

1½ cups shredded cheddar cheese (6 ounces)

1. Preheat the oven to 400°F. Place the tortillas in the bowl of a food processor and pulse until the tortillas are pulverized into fine crumbs. Add the flour and ¼ teaspoon of the salt and pulse to combine. With the motor running, drizzle in the vegetable oil and then the water and process until the mixture forms a clumpy dough.

2. Turn the dough out into a 9-inch nonstick pie pan and press the dough evenly into the bottom and sides of the pan. Bake until the crust begins to brown on the sides and it feels dry to the touch, 10 to 15 minutes.

3. In a bowl, whisk together the eggs, cream, milk, the remaining ¼ teaspoon salt, and the pepper. Arrange the broccoli in an even layer in the crust. Sprinkle half of the cheese over the broccoli.

Pour the filling over the broccoli and cheese, and sprinkle the remaining cheese over the filling. Bake the quiche until it is no longer jiggly in the middle, 30 to 35 minutes. Serve hot or at room temperature.

· · · · · · · · ·

KALE QUESADILLAS WITH TOMATILLO SAUCE

I love chopped kale in quesadillas—the sturdy green wilts just enough to be tender, but still retains a nice crisp texture. With a tart tomatillo sauce for dipping, these quesadillas make a great summer or fall meal.

Serves 4

1 pound tomatillos, husked and quartered

1 jalapeño, seeded, chopped

juice of 1 lime (about 2 tablespoons)

¼ cup fresh cilantro

¼ teaspoon kosher salt

8 small (6-inch) flour tortillas

1½ cups shredded Monterey Jack cheese (6 ounces)

1 cup chopped kale

1. In a blender, combine the tomatillos, jalapeño, lime juice, cilantro leaves, and salt. Blend until relatively smooth. Pour into a serving dish, cover, and refrigerate until needed.

2. To make the quesadillas, sprinkle a few tablespoons of cheese on 4 of the tortillas. Add about ¼ cup chopped kale on each tortilla. Divide the remaining cheese between the tortillas, sprinkling on top of the kale. Top with the remaining 4 tortillas. Cook the quesadillas on a dry skillet or griddle, about 2 to 3 minutes on each side, until tortillas are crisp and lightly browned and the cheese is melted. To serve, cut the quesadillas into wedges and either drizzle the sauce over the quesadillas or serve it in individual bowls for dipping.

• • • • • • • •

TORTILLA-CRUSTED EGGPLANT WITH SPICY TOMATO SAUCE

This is a Southwestern interpretation of eggplant Parmesan. Crunchy tortilla chips make the eggplant's breading, while the red pepper flakes give the tomato sauce a kick. **Serves 4**

1 large eggplant

½ cup all-purpose flour

2 large eggs, lightly beaten

6 cups tortilla chips (about 6 ounces)

1 tablespoon vegetable oil, plus more for frying

1 small yellow onion, diced

1 (15-ounce) jar tomato sauce

2 teaspoons red pepper flakes

1 pound fresh mozzarella cheese, sliced

kosher salt and black pepper

1. Line a rimmed baking sheet with paper towels. Slice the eggplant about ¾ inch thick, discarding both ends. Generously sprinkle both sides of each slice with salt and place on the prepared baking sheet. Place a second baking sheet on top of the eggplant and weigh it down with a few cans of food. Let sit for 20 minutes, allowing the weighted baking sheet to press the bitter juices out of the eggplant. Rinse the eggplant slices and pat dry.

2. Place the flour in a pie pan or shallow dish, and the beaten eggs in a second pan or dish. Place the tortilla chips in a zip-top plastic bag and crush with your hands, a rolling pin, or a saucepan into fine crumbs. Pour the chips into a third pie pan or shallow dish. Bread the eggplant pieces by dredging first in the flour, patting the excess flour off, then dipping in the egg, and dredging in the crushed tortilla chips. Try to use one hand to handle the dry ingredients and the other for the egg, to avoid your hands getting too messy. Place the breaded eggplants on a tray or a baking sheet and let rest for 20 minutes to allow the breading to set.

3. While the eggplant is resting, make the sauce: Heat the 1 tablespoon vegetable oil in a medium saucepan over medium heat. Add the onion and cook, stirring occasionally, until softened and translucent, about 5 minutes. Add the sauce and the red pepper flakes, bring to a simmer, then reduce heat to low and simmer for 5 to 10 minutes to allow the flavors to blend. Season to taste with salt and pepper. Turn off the heat and cover to keep warm.

4. Preheat the oven's broiler and line a rimmed baking sheet with paper towels. Pour vegetable oil into a skillet to a depth of about ½ inch and heat over medium-high heat until the oil shimmers. Working in batches to avoid overcrowding, fry the eggplant until the outside is crisp and the eggplant looks softened, about 3 minutes per side, turning over when the underside is golden. Transfer the fried eggplant to the prepared baking sheet.

5. Arrange the eggplant in a 9 x 13-inch glass baking dish. Spoon some spicy tomato sauce over each eggplant and top with a slice of cheese. Broil for 3 to 4 minutes or until the cheese is bubbly and melted. Serve hot.

· · · · · · · · ·

MUSHROOM TART

The earthiness of the mushrooms in this elegant tart is a nice foil for the mellow flavor of the tortilla crust. It makes a great light supper or an appetizer for a dinner party. I use a combination of inexpensive cremini mushrooms and pricier but more interesting varieties, like shiitakes and chanterelles. **Serves 8**

7 small (6-inch) corn tortillas

½ teaspoon kosher salt, divided

3 tablespoons unsalted butter, divided

¼ cup warm water

1 medium shallot, minced

12 ounces assorted mushrooms, chopped

1 tablespoon chopped fresh thyme or ½ teaspoon dried thyme

1 large egg

¾ cup heavy cream

¼ cup finely grated Parmesan cheese (1 ounce)

1. Preheat the oven to 350°F. Tear the tortillas into pieces and place in the bowl of a food processor. Process until the tortillas are ground into fine crumbs. Add ¼ teaspoon of the salt and pulse to combine. In a small microwave-safe bowl, melt 2 tablespoons of the butter. With the motor running, drizzle the butter into the food processor, then add enough warm water until the mixture makes a clumpy dough. Turn out into a 9-inch tart pan with a removable base, and press the dough evenly into the bottom and sides of the pan. Being careful to lift the tart pan from the sides, rather than the bottom, place the pan on a rimmed baking sheet, put the baking sheet in the oven, and bake until the crust is beginning to turn golden and is dry to the touch, about 20 minutes.

2. While the crust is baking, melt the remaining 1 tablespoon butter in a large skillet over medium-low heat. Add the shallots and cook, stirring frequently, until soft and translucent, about 4 minutes. Add the mushrooms. Cook, stirring frequently, until the mushrooms are very soft and any water they release is evaporated, about 7 to 9 minutes. Sprinkle the thyme and the remaining ¼ teaspoon salt over the mushrooms and remove from the heat. Whisk the egg in a medium bowl. Whisk in the cream and the Parmesan cheese. Stir the cream mixture into the mushrooms, and spoon the mushroom and cream mixture into the prepared tart crust. Return to the oven and bake until set, 20 to 25 minutes. Serve hot, warm, or at room temperature.

· · · · · · · · ·

SPICY TOFU WRAPS

Strips of seasoned tofu fill these wraps for a satisfying alternative to grilled meat. Creamy avocado and crisp lettuce are the perfect accompaniments, along with your favorite salsa. **Serves 4**

1 (15-ounce) block extra-firm tofu

½ teaspoon ground cumin

1 teaspoon red chile powder

¼ teaspoon kosher salt

juice of 1 lime (about 2 tablespoons)

2 teaspoons vegetable oil

4 medium (8-inch) flour tortillas

1 small head green leaf lettuce, shredded

1 medium avocado, pitted, peeled, and sliced

½ cup prepared salsa

1. Press the tofu under a weighted plate or in a tofu press for 30 minutes to 1 hour, to squeeze out excess water and give the tofu a firmer texture. In a small bowl, combine the cumin, red chile powder, and salt. Cut the tofu in half lengthwise, then slice crosswise into ¾-inch strips. Place the tofu in a bowl, drizzle with the lime juice, and sprinkle with the seasonings, tossing to coat.

2. Heat the vegetable oil in a medium nonstick skillet over medium-high heat. Use tongs to place the tofu strips into the skillet. Cook for 12 to 15 minutes, turning the tofu pieces over with the tongs every 3 to 4 minutes to evenly brown all sides.

3. To serve, warm the tortillas over a burner or stacked in the microwave on high power for 20 seconds. Divide the tofu between the tortillas, garnish with lettuce and avocado slices, and drizzle with about 2 tablespoons each salsa. Wrap like burritos (see page 75) and serve warm.

· · · · · · · · ·

PORTOBELLO, RED PEPPER, AND GOAT CHEESE FAJITAS

These veggie fajitas have a Mediterranean vibe since they're marinated in balsamic vinegar and wrapped up with creamy goat cheese. It's an easy weeknight meal that's big on flavor! **Serves 4**

¼ cup balsamic vinegar

1 tablespoon extra-virgin olive oil

½ teaspoon kosher salt

2 medium red bell peppers, seeds removed, sliced

1 large red onion, halved and sliced

2 large portobello mushrooms, gills scraped away, sliced

1 tablespoon vegetable oil

4 medium (8-inch) flour tortillas

4 ounces goat cheese, softened

1. In a large bowl, combine the vinegar, olive oil, and salt. Add the peppers, onion, and mushrooms and marinate for 10 minutes, tossing occasionally with tongs to coat the vegetables evenly with the marinade.

2. Add the vegetable oil to a grill pan or large skillet and heat over high heat. Lifting the vegetables out of the marinade with tongs, add them to the skillet. Cook for 10 minutes, turning and stirring occasionally with the tongs, until softened and lightly browned. Warm the tortillas over an open burner for about 10 seconds on each side or stack and microwave on high power for 20 seconds. Sprinkle goat cheese over the middle of each warmed tortilla, divide the cooked fajita vegetables among the tortillas, and wrap the tortillas around the filling.

• • • • • • • •

CHILE RELLENO TACOS

Chile rellenos are messy and involved to make, but they're well worth it. I like to eat them wrapped up in a fresh flour tortilla. If you want to spread out the work, roast the chiles up to a day before making this meal, and store them in a lidded container or a zip-top bag. You can find the traditional Chihuahua cheese for making chiles rellenos in a Hispanic grocer or in the cheese case or international aisle of your supermarket. **Serves 6**

6 fresh poblano chiles

6 ounces quesadilla cheese or Chihuahua cheese, cut into 6 long strips

1 cup all-purpose flour, divided

½ teaspoon baking powder

½ teaspoon baking soda

1 large egg

½ cup milk

vegetable oil, as needed

1 teaspoon kosher salt

4 medium (8-inch) flour tortillas

1. To roast the chiles, working in batches, place the chiles over the flame of a burner until blackened completely, turning them as they cook to evenly blacken all sides. Alternatively, place the chiles on a baking sheet and roast under the broiler, checking every few minutes and turning the chiles to roast all sides evenly. Immediately place the hot chiles in a heatproof bowl and cover tightly with plastic wrap. Let steam in the bowl for about 15 minutes to give the steam a chance to loosen the blackened skin. When the chiles are cool enough to touch, peel off the blackened skin, rubbing the skin off under running water if needed.

2. Cut a small slit in the side of each chile and stuff a piece of cheese into each.

3. In a medium bowl, combine ½ cup of the flour and the baking powder and baking soda, stirring with a whisk or a fork to combine. In a second medium bowl, beat the egg with the fork or whisk. Whisk in the milk, and then gradually stir in the dry ingredients to make a batter. Place the remaining ½ cup flour in a shallow bowl or plate.

4. Line a plate with paper towels. Heat about 1 inch of vegetable oil in a large skillet over high heat until it shimmers. Dredge a pepper in flour, dusting off the excess flour, then dip in the batter, holding from the stem. Place the chile in the hot oil; the pepper should immediately begin sizzling when it comes in contact with the hot oil. Repeat with two or three other peppers to fill the pan without overcrowding. Cook until the underside is golden, 1 to 2 minutes, then carefully turn over with a slotted metal spoon and cook on the second side until golden, 1 to 2 minutes longer. Transfer to the paper towel–lined plate and sprinkle lightly with salt. Repeat with the remaining chiles.

5. Warm the flour tortillas over an open burner for about 10 seconds on each side or stack and microwave on high power for 20 seconds. Wrap a warm tortilla around each cooked pepper. Serve immediately.

• • • • • • • • •

TORTILLA PIZZAS WITH MEATLESS CRUMBLES

Flour tortillas make a crisp, no-fuss crust for mock pizzas. Use your favorite toppings to make a tasty lunch or dinner, paired with a Caesar salad. **Serves 4**

4 medium (8-inch) flour tortillas

1 tablespoon extra-virgin olive oil

1 tablespoon vegetable oil

8 ounces sausage-style meatless crumbles

1 cup marinara sauce

1 (4-ounce) can sliced black olives, drained

1 cup shredded mozzarella cheese (4 ounces)

1. Preheat the oven to 425°F. Brush the tortillas on both sides with olive oil. Arrange the tortillas on two rimmed baking sheets and prick all over with a fork. Bake until crisp, about 10 minutes, turning the tortillas over once and switching the pans if they're on two oven racks.

2. While the tortillas are baking, heat the vegetable oil in a medium skillet over medium heat. Add the meatless crumbles and cook, stirring occasionally, until heated through, 6 to 8 minutes.

3. Spread each pizza with about ¼ cup marinara sauce. Top with some of the crumbles and the black olives. Sprinkle with the cheese. Return the pans to the oven and bake until the cheese melts, 4 to 5 minutes. Cut into quarters and serve hot.

· · · · · · · · ·

TUX-WORTHY TORTILLAS

Tortillas don't always have to be the stuff of college kids' cheap meals and easy game day party fare. Indeed, with the right ingredients and a more thoughtful presentation, you can elevate them to a higher culinary realm. Serve these creative and exotic dishes for your favorite gourmets or at your next dinner party—they're sure to impress!

FIG AND GOAT CHEESE PINWHEELS

These treats make for an unexpected treat on any appetizer buffet. Even though they only have three ingredients and they're supereasy to prepare, they always draw rave reviews when I serve them at parties, and they're usually one of the first appetizer platters to empty! **Makes 24 pinwheel bites**

3 medium (8-inch) flour tortillas

5 ounces goat cheese, softened

1 cup chopped dried figs (6 to 7 ounces)

1. Preheat the oven to 350°F. Line a rimmed baking sheet with parchment paper. Stack the tortillas and microwave on high power until soft and pliable, about 20 seconds. Spread the goat cheese over the tortillas, leaving about ¾ inch on one end of each tortilla uncovered. Sprinkle the figs over the goat cheese. Roll the tortilla tightly around the filling, ending with the uncovered side, being careful not to squeeze the filling out of the ends.

2. Place the rolls on the prepared baking sheet and bake until warmed and the tortillas are beginning to get crispy, about 10 minutes. Let cool on the baking sheet for a few minutes, then use a sharp serrated knife to cut the rolls into roughly 8 (1-inch) pinwheels. Serve warm.

. . . .

WILD MUSHROOM FLATBREADS WITH TRUFFLE CHEESE

Truffles elevate any fare to haute cuisine, even a fancified version of pizza. In this recipe, exotic mushrooms and truffle cheese top crisped tortillas to make a delicious flatbread that's good for an appetizer, a party hors d'oeuvre, or even a light supper with a salad. Check for truffle-infused cheese at your local cheese shop. There are several different varieties, but they're typically a semisoft, mild white cheese that's studded with truffle shavings and flavored with oil. Truffle cheese is often called by its original Italian names, sottocenere or perla grigia; Mémoire is a popular brand. **Serves 2 as an entree, 6 as an appetizer (makes 2 flatbreads)**

2 medium (8-inch) flour tortillas

2 tablespoons extra-virgin olive oil, divided

12 ounces assorted exotic mushrooms, such as cremini, chanterelle, shiitake, or hen-of-the-woods

1 cup shredded truffle-infused cheese (4 ounces)

1. Preheat the oven to 375°F. Brush the tortillas on both sides with 1 tablespoon of the olive oil and place on a rimmed baking sheet. Prick all over with a fork and bake until the tortillas are crisp and lightly browned, about 10 minutes, turning over halfway through cooking,

2. Meanwhile, in a skillet, heat the remaining 1 tablespoon olive oil over medium-low heat. Add the mushrooms and cook, stirring occasionally, until they are very soft and any liquid they've released has evaporated, 7 to 9 minutes.

3. Spread the mushrooms on the baked tortillas and sprinkle with the cheese. Return the tortillas to the oven and bake until the cheese has melted, 7 to 9 minutes. Let cool a few minutes before cutting into slices or wedges with a knife or a pizza wheel. Serve warm.

. . . .

SCALLOPS ON CRISPED TORTILLAS WITH CHIPOTLE CREAM SAUCE

This dish is all about luxury—perfectly seared scallops (which I think are among the most elegant of seafood choices), a velvety cream sauce delicately flavored with smoky chipotle, and the crunch of a crispy tortilla. Serve just one on a tiny plate for a memorable beginning to a meal. **Makes 8**

2 small (6-inch) flour tortillas

3 tablespoons unsalted butter, divided

2 tablespoons all-purpose flour

¾ cup whole milk

½ cup heavy cream

⅛ teaspoon garlic powder

½ teaspoon ground chipotle powder

2 tablespoons dry white wine or vermouth

1 teaspoon white wine vinegar

1 tablespoon vegetable oil

8 large sea scallops (about 1 pound)

kosher salt and black pepper

8 small sprigs cilantro, for garnish

1. Preheat the oven to 375°F. Cut the tortillas into quarters (for 8 pieces total), place on a baking sheet, and prick all over with a fork. Bake until crisp, about 10 minutes. Remove from the oven and let cool on the baking sheet.

2. In a medium saucepan, melt 2 tablespoons of the butter over medium heat. When it foams, add the flour and whisk until it forms a clumpy paste. Gradually whisk in the milk until smooth. Bring the mixture to a simmer, then reduce heat to low and stir in the cream. Simmer until the mixture has thickened enough to coat the back of a spoon, 7 to 10 minutes. Stir in the garlic powder, chipotle powder, white wine, and vinegar. Season to taste with salt and pepper.

3. Pat the scallops dry and season both sides with salt and pepper. Heat the vegetable oil and remaining 1 tablespoon butter in a large skillet over medium-high heat. Add the scallops to the pan and cook until the underside is opaque and browned, 4 to 5 minutes. Turn the scallops over and cook on the second side until browned, 4 to 5 minutes. Arrange the tortilla crisps on a platter or individual appetizer plates, top each with a scallop, and drizzle with the sauce. Top each with a sprig of cilantro.

• • • • • • • •

COFFEE-BRAISED SHORT RIB TACOS

Short ribs braised with all sorts of interesting ingredients are popping up on upscale restaurant menus every time I turn around, so I decided to try my hand at using this rich, flavorful cut as a taco filling. No one will be able to tell that coffee is the secret ingredient in the braising sauce; it just adds a rich, mellow note of flavor alongside the tomato paste and smoky chipotle. The short ribs cook all afternoon, perfuming the air with the delicious aroma—perfect for a lazy winter day. **Serves 4 (makes 8 tacos)**

2½ pounds short ribs

1 tablespoon vegetable oil

1 small yellow onion, diced

2 medium carrots, peeled and sliced

2 ribs celery, diced

1 (6-ounce) can tomato paste

2 cups black coffee

2 teaspoons ground chipotle

8 small (6-inch) corn tortillas

2 ounces baby arugula

4 radishes, thinly sliced

1 lime, cut into wedges, for serving

kosher salt

1. Preheat the oven to 350°F. Season the ribs with salt. In an ovenproof skillet, heat the vegetable oil over medium-high heat. Add the ribs and cook until browned, 5 to 6 minutes on each side, turning the pieces over and on their sides to brown all the exposed meat. The process should take 15 to 20 minutes total.

2. Transfer the meat to a platter. Add the onion, carrots, and celery to the pan and cook over medium heat, stirring occasionally, until the vegetables are tender and the onion is translucent, about 10 minutes. Add the tomato paste and stir it into the vegetables, cooking until it begins to brown, about 10 minutes. Return the meat to the pan and add the coffee and chipotle powder. Bring to a simmer. Cover the pan and place it in the oven. Cook for 1 hour. Take the pan out of the oven, turn over the meant, and cook 45 minutes longer. Uncover the pan and cook 30 minutes longer, to allow the liquid to reduce slightly.

3. Remove the meat from the pan and let cool slightly. Strip the meat from the bone, chop or shred it into pieces, and place it in a serving bowl. Stir in just enough of the cooking liquid to moisten the meat, and season to taste with salt.

4. Warm the tortillas in a dry skillet for about 10 seconds on each side or stacked in the microwave on high power for 20 seconds. Make the tacos by placing meat, arugula, and radish slices in a tortilla and topping with a squeeze of lime. Serve immediately.

· · · · · · · · ·

DUCK QUESADILLA WITH AVOCADO CREAM

Years ago at a party, my friend Grace served quesadillas that were filled with duck and goat cheese and accompanied by an addictive avocado dip. It was the first time I'd ever tasted duck, and the rich meat coupled with the creamy, tangy dip was so memorable that I still think of it from time to time. This recipe is as close as I can come to re-creating Grace's wonderful quesadillas, which she says were from an old Sheila Lukins cookbook. Serve them as a main course, or do like Grace did, and pass them at a party. **Makes 4 quesadillas**

1 medium avocado	8 medium (8-inch) flour tortillas
½ cup sour cream	4 ounces goat cheese
juice of 1 lime (about 2 tablespoons)	1 cup shredded fontina cheese (4 ounces)
2 (6-ounce) duck breasts	kosher salt and black pepper
8 ounces sliced cremini mushrooms	

1. Cut the avocado in half, remove the pit, and scoop the flesh into a medium bowl. Add the sour cream and the lime juice, and use an immersion blender to puree the ingredients into a smooth sauce. Season to taste with salt and pepper. Refrigerate, covered, until needed.

2. Preheat the oven to 350°F. Line a rimmed baking sheet with aluminum foil. Score the fatty layer of the duck breast by slicing into the fat in a crisscross pattern with a knife, making cuts about ¾ inch apart. Season both sides of the duck breasts with salt and pepper. Heat a medium skillet over medium-high heat. Add the duck, fat-side down, and cook, undisturbed, until the fat has rendered off, about 5 minutes. Turn the breast over and cook on the second side until browned, 2 to 3 minutes longer. Transfer the breasts to the prepared baking sheet and roast in the oven for 5 to 7 minutes, until the internal temperature of the meat registers 165°F when checked with a meat thermometer. Let the meat rest until it's cool enough to handle, then chop the duck into small pieces.

3. While the duck is cooking, drain and discard, or save for another use, all but about 1 tablespoon of the fat from the pan in which the duck was cooked. Return the pan to the stove over medium heat and add the mushrooms. Cook, stirring occasionally, until the mushrooms are very soft and the liquid they release has evaporated, 6 to 8 minutes. Season to taste with salt and pepper.

4. Spread the goat cheese in a thin layer on the tortillas. Distribute the mushrooms and duck evenly over 4 of the tortillas, and sprinkle about ¼ cup of fontina cheese over each. Place the other tortillas, goat cheese on the inside, on top of the fontina cheese.

5. Heat a large dry skillet over medium-high heat. Add one quesadilla to the pan, and toast until the cheese is melted and the outside of the tortilla is lightly browned, 2 to 3 minutes. Turn over and toast the other side, 2 to 3 minutes longer. Repeat with the remaining quesadillas. To serve, slice the quesadillas in wedges and serve with the avocado cream sauce for dipping.

· · · · · · · · ·

ROASTED VEGETABLE NAPOLEONS

Corn tortillas are stacked between roasted vegetables and nutty Parmesan cheese in this elegant dish that makes a great upscale option for a vegetarian dinner party. This dish is especially nice to make in the summer, when these vegetables are at their peak. Cutting rounds out of the tortillas gives the dish a lovely presentation; be sure to save the scraps to use in another recipe, such as in the crust of a Mushroom Tart (page 120) or a Pineapple Cheesecake (page 174). **Serves 4**

4 ounces crème fraîche

2 tablespoons minced fresh chives

¼ cup plus 1 tablespoon extra-virgin olive oil, divided

1 large globe tomato, cut into four slices

1 medium zucchini, sliced

1 bunch arugula, coarsely chopped (about 4 ounces)

vegetable oil, for frying

12 small (6-inch) corn tortillas

½ cup finely grated Parmesan cheese (2 ounces)

kosher salt and black pepper

1. Preheat the oven to 450°F. Line two rimmed baking sheets with parchment paper. In a small bowl, stir together the crème fraîche, chives, and about ¼ teaspoon salt. Cover and refrigerate until needed.

2. Pour ¼ cup of the olive oil in a small dish. Place the tomato slices on one prepared baking sheet. Brush each side with the olive oil and season lightly with salt and pepper. Place the zucchini slices on the second prepared baking sheet and brush both sides of each slice with olive oil and season with salt and pepper. Place the baking sheets in the oven on the middle and bottom racks and roast until the vegetables are soft, 10 to 15 minutes, switching rack positions after about 7 minutes.

3. In a small skillet, heat 1 tablespoon of the olive oil over medium heat. Add the arugula and cook, turning over occasionally with tongs, until wilted, 3 to 4 minutes. Season to taste with salt and pepper and transfer to a bowl.

4. Line a plate with paper towels. Wipe out the skillet, then fill with about ½ inch of vegetable oil. Using a 3-inch metal biscuit cutter, cut circles out of each tortilla (reserve the scraps for another use). Fry the rounds in the oil until crisp, about 30 seconds on each side. Transfer to the paper towel-lined plate to drain off the excess oil.

5. To assemble, place 1 tortilla round on a plate. Top with a little arugula and a sprinkling of Parmesan cheese. Place another tortilla on the arugula, and top with a tomato slice and more Parmesan. Place a third tortilla on the tomato, and top with a couple of zucchini pieces and more Parmesan cheese. Repeat with the remaining tortillas, vegetables, and cheese. Garnish each with a dollop of the crème fraîche–chive mixture. Serve warm.

● ● ● ● ● ● ● ● ●

SALMON CAVIAR AND EDAMAME BITES

Back when I used to cater friends' parties in New York City, I prepared a version of this for a birthday party where the theme was "indulgence." The guests loved how colorful and elegant the presentation was. Salmon roe is not as expensive as true caviar from sturgeon, and a little goes a long way, but to me this recipe seems extravagant and luxurious. If you need to do some work in advance, bake the tortilla shells and make and refrigerate the edamame puree earlier in the day or the day before, but assemble the bites shortly before guests arrive so that the tortillas stay crisp. **Makes 1 dozen**

1 large (10 to 12-inch) flour tortilla

1 tablespoon plus 1 teaspoon sesame oil

1 tablespoon sesame seeds

1 (10-ounce) package frozen shelled edamame

1 teaspoon wasabi paste

1 tablespoon freshly squeezed lemon juice

1 (4-ounce) tin salmon roe

1. Preheat the oven to 350°F. Brush the both sides of the tortilla with 1 tablespoon of the sesame oil. Using a 1½-inch or 2-inch metal biscuit cutter, cut out about 12 rounds. Place the rounds on a rimmed baking sheet and prick all over with a fork. Sprinkle with the sesame seeds. Bake until the rounds are crisp, 10 to 12 minutes, turning over halfway through cooking. Let cool completely on the baking sheet.

2. Cook the edamame according to the package directions. Drain the excess water and transfer the edamame to the bowl

COMFORTING CASSEROLES

Who doesn't love a casserole? There's not much not to like: They're generally easy to prepare, substantial and comforting to eat, and make enough to share with a crowd or have leftovers. One of my favorite things about casseroles is that they generally spend half an hour or so in the oven before they're ready to eat, which gives you plenty of time to clean up the kitchen and throw together a salad or a side dish before sitting down to the table. In these recipes, tortillas are torn, layered, and ground to add their distinctive flavor and hearty texture to a variety of dishes.

CHILAQUILES CASSEROLE

Chilaquiles are perhaps the original Mexican casserole—the dish always include tortillas (usually stale ones or leftovers), but beyond that, anything goes. There's generally eggs or chicken, and typically it's all mixed together in salsa or a tomato sauce. My version includes all of the above, which in my mind makes it suitable for any time of day, from breakfast through dinner. In fact, since some people say it has hangover-curing properties, I can imagine this dish would even be a good late-night nosh after an evening of carousing. Look for queso fresco cheese in the international aisle or in the cheese section of a grocery store. It's a mild, crumbly white cheese. **Serves 8**

2 tablespoons vegetable oil

8 small (6-inch) corn tortillas, cut into wedges

8 large eggs

1 (12-ounce) jar prepared salsa

¾ pound cooked chicken, skin removed, shredded

1 (4-ounce) can black olives, drained

6 ounces crumbled queso fresco

1. Preheat the oven to 350°F. In a large ovenproof skillet, heat the vegetable oil over medium-high heat. Add the tortillas and cook until they begin to get crispy, 8 to 10 minutes. Reduce the heat to low, add the eggs, and cook, stirring with a spatula, until the eggs are scrambled but still moist, 2 to 3 minutes. Stir in the salsa, chicken, and black olives. Stir to combine all the ingredients, and smooth to make an even layer in the pan. Sprinkle with the queso fresco. Transfer to the oven and bake until the cheese is melted, about 20 minutes. Serve hot.

• • • • • • • • •

GREENS 'N' BEANS PIE

I was inspired to create this recipe when I had a bunch of extra kale from another dish I'd made, and it's quickly become one of my family's favorites. It's quick to assemble and, other than the greens, is made with staples you probably already have on hand. A not-too-chunky salsa is best; I use a mild version when I'm serving this to kids but it's excellent with a spicier blend for adults. **Serves 4**

1 tablespoon vegetable oil

1 small onion, diced

8 cups chopped kale or spinach (about 6½ ounces)

8 small (6-inch) corn tortillas

1 (16-ounce) jar prepared salsa

1½ cups canned black beans, drained and rinsed

2 cups shredded Colby Jack cheese (about 5 ounces)

1. Preheat the oven to 375°F. Heat the vegetable oil in a large skillet over medium-high heat. Add the onion and cook, stirring occasionally, until softened, 5 to 7 minutes. Add the kale or spinach and cook, stirring occasionally, until wilted, 4 to 5 minutes, using tongs to turn the greens over in the pan so they cook evenly.

2. To assemble the pie, spray a 9-inch pie pan with cooking spray. Line the base of the pan with tortillas, tearing the tortillas into large pieces to fit and cover the entire bottom of the pan. Spread about ¼ cup salsa over the tortillas. Sprinkle about one-third of the beans over the salsa, followed by about one-third of the greens. Sprinkle one-third of the cheese evenly over the beans and greens. Repeat with the remaining ingredients twice, to make three layers, ending with cheese. Press down on the top of the pie with the back of a spoon to compress it slightly.

3. Bake until the cheese is melted and bubbling, 15 to 20 minutes. Cut into wedges and serve hot.

• • • • • • • • •

EASIEST ENCHILADA BAKE

There are only five ingredients in this casserole, and it'll just take a few minutes to assemble, perfect for a busy weeknight or unexpected guests. Of course, you're welcome to make it fancier or more complicated. Consider mixing cheese types, using homemade enchilada sauce, or adding cooked, chopped veggies to the filling. Or, use cooked ground beef or turkey, shredded beef, or meatless crumbles in place of the chicken. If this is a main course, anticipate two enchiladas per person, but at a potluck, most people will just take one. **Makes 8 to 10 enchiladas**

2 (10-ounce) cans enchilada sauce or about 2½ cups homemade red chile sauce

8 to 10 small (6-inch) corn tortillas

2 cups shredded Colby cheese (8 ounces)

1 pound cooked chicken, shredded

1 (4-ounce) can sliced black olives, drained

1. Preheat the oven to 375°F. Pour a little enchilada sauce into a 9 x 13-inch glass baking dish to cover the bottom. Pour the remaining sauce into a shallow bowl.

2. To make the enchiladas, dip a tortilla in the sauce to coat completely and set on a clean work surface like a cutting board or plate. Sprinkle about 1 tablespoon of cheese in a line down the center of the tortilla, then add a handful of chicken and a few black olives. Roll the tortilla and place it in the baking dish with edge of the tortilla on the bottom to prevent it from opening. Finish with the remaining tortillas to make 8 or 10 enchiladas, depending on how you fill them, lining up the enchiladas in a row in the dish.

3. Pour the remaining sauce over the tortillas and sprinkle them with the remaining cheese. Bake until heated through and the cheese is melted, 20 to 25 minutes. Serve hot or warm.

• • • • • • • •

MEXICAN LASAGNA

I hate working with lasagna noodles—the kind you have to boil first always seem to tear, and the no-bake versions often end up with hard, crunchy bits. So I was thrilled one day when I was out of lasagna noodles and decided to try making a lasagna-type casserole with corn tortillas instead. Surprisingly, the end result didn't taste much different than if I'd made the dish with noodles, but I added some Mexican flavor elements to give it a Southwestern twist. **Serves 8**

1 tablespoon extra-virgin olive oil

1 medium onion, diced

2 cloves garlic, minced

1 (28-ounce) can crushed tomatoes

2 teaspoons ground cumin

½ teaspoon chipotle powder

1 teaspoon kosher salt, divided

¼ teaspoon ground black pepper, divided

1¼ pounds Italian sausage (turkey or pork), casings removed

1 large egg

1 (15-ounce) container ricotta cheese

¼ cup plus 2 tablespoons finely grated Parmesan cheese, divided

10 small (6-inch) corn tortillas, or as needed

1 pound frozen chopped spinach, thawed, excess water squeezed out

2½ cups shredded part-skim mozzarella cheese (1 pound)

1. Preheat the oven to 375°F. In a large saucepan, heat the olive oil over medium-high heat. Add the onion and cook, stirring occasionally, until softened and translucent, 5 to 7 minutes. Add the garlic and cook, stirring frequently, for 30 seconds. Add the tomatoes, cumin, chipotle powder, ½ teaspoon of the salt, and ⅛ teaspoon of the pepper. Bring to a simmer, then reduce the heat to low and cook, stirring occasionally, for 10 minutes. Remove from heat, and let cool slightly.

2. In a large nonstick skillet, cook the sausage over medium heat, breaking it up into small chunks, until browned through, about 7 minutes. Remove from heat, drain the excess fat, and set aside.

3. While the tomato sauce and sausage are cooking, lightly beat the egg in a medium bowl. Stir in the ricotta cheese, ¼ cup of the Parmesan cheese, the remaining ½ teaspoon salt, and the remaining ⅛ teaspoon pepper.

4. Spray a medium baking dish (about 11 x 7 inches) with cooking spray. Spread a spoonful of tomato sauce over the bottom of the pan. Dip 3 tortillas in the cooled tomato sauce and, tearing to fit, line the bottom of the pan. Spread about half the ricotta cheese mixture over the tortillas, then sprinkle with half of the spinach, half of the sausage, and about 1 cup of the mozzarella cheese. Create more layers with more dipped tortillas torn to cover the mozzarella cheese, the remaining ricotta cheese mixture, and the sausage and spinach. Sprinkle with 1 cup of the mozzarella cheese. Create a third layer of dipped tortillas. Spoon the remaining sauce over the tortillas to cover, sprinkle with the remaining ½ cup mozzarella cheese and the remaining 2 tablespoons Parmesan cheese. Bake until the sauce is bubbling and the cheese is melted, 40 to 50 minutes. Serve hot.

• • • • • • • • •

SHRIMP AND BLACK BEAN CASSEROLE

Use your favorite salsa—hot or mild—to moisten this casserole. **Serves 6 to 8**

1 pound medium shrimp, peeled, deveined, and tails removed

1 medium green bell pepper, diced

2 (15-ounce) cans black beans, drained and rinsed

1 (16-ounce) package frozen corn, thawed

6 small (6-inch) corn tortillas, cut or torn into 1-inch squares

1 (16-ounce) jar prepared salsa

2 cups shredded Colby cheese or Mexican cheese blend (8 ounces)

1. Preheat the oven to 350°F. Spray a 9 x 13-inch glass baking dish with cooking spray or brush lightly with vegetable oil. In a large bowl, mix together the shrimp, bell pepper, beans, corn, tortillas, salsa, and 1 cup of the cheese. Spread the mixture into the prepared dish, smoothing with a spatula to even it out. Sprinkle with the remaining 1 cup cheese. Bake until the shrimp are opaque and the cheese is melted, about 30 minutes.

. . . .

BURRITO CASSEROLE

All the best parts of a burrito are in this casserole: beans, meat, brown rice, cheese, salsa, sour cream, and avocado. It's a great dish to take to a potluck, as it has wide appeal. You can make this with ground beef, ground turkey, or even meatless crumbles depending on your taste. If the casserole will be sitting out for a while after baking, omit the avocado, as it will quickly turn brown. **Serves 12**

1 tablespoon vegetable oil

1 small onion, diced

1¼ pounds ground beef or turkey

1 tablespoon taco seasoning

6 small (6-inch) corn tortillas

1 (15-ounce) can refried beans

1½ cups cooked brown rice

12 ounces prepared salsa

1½ cups shredded Colby Jack cheese (6 ounces)

¾ cup sour cream

1 medium avocado, pitted, peeled, and diced

1. Preheat the oven to 350°F. Spray a 9 x 13-inch glass baking dish with cooking spray or brush lightly with vegetable oil.

2. Heat the vegetable oil in a large nonstick skillet over medium heat. Add the onion and cook, stirring occasionally, until soft and translucent, about 5 minutes. Increase the heat to medium-high and add the meat, breaking into small pieces with a wooden spoon, and cook until browned and cooked through, about 10 minutes. Stir in the taco seasoning.

3. In the prepared baking dish, layer the tortillas so that they overlap and fold slightly up the sides of the dish. Spread the beans over the tortillas. Sprinkle the rice in an even layer over the beans. Spread the meat over the rice, and pour the salsa into the pan, using a spoon or a spatula to spread it over the meat layer. Sprinkle with the cheese and bake until the cheese is melted and the layers are heated through, about 30 minutes.

4. Evenly space 12 dollops of sour cream on the casserole, three rows across and four rows the length of the pan. Sprinkle a few pieces of avocado on top of the sour cream. The dollops will help provide a guideline for cutting 12 equal pieces of the casserole. Serve hot or warm.

• • • • • • • •

SPICY CHICKEN CASSEROLE

Ro*Tel is a canned product that combines diced tomatoes and green chiles. It was first created in Texas in the 1940s, and is still most commonly available in the South, but you might be able to find it with the canned goods in a well-stocked supermarket. If you can't track it down, use a 15-ounce can of diced tomatoes and a 4-ounce can of diced green chiles. This casserole is a great way to use up leftover chicken, or you can simply pull the meat off a rotisserie chicken from the supermarket. **Serves 6 to 8**

2 (10-ounce) cans Ro*Tel Diced Tomatoes and Green Chiles

8 ounces cream cheese, cut into cubes

1 pound cooked boneless, skinless chicken, cut into chunks

1 (16-ounce) bag frozen cut green beans, thawed

6 small (6-inch) corn tortillas, torn into pieces

1 cup shredded Colby cheese (4 ounces)

1. Preheat the oven to 350°F. Spray a 9 x 13-inch glass baking dish with cooking spray or brush lightly with vegetable oil. In a large saucepan, heat the Ro*Tel over low heat until just simmering. Add the cream cheese and stir until the cheese is melted and the mixture is smooth and creamy. Stir in the chicken, green beans, and tortillas.

2. Spoon the mixture into the prepared casserole dish. Sprinkle evenly with the cheese. Bake until heated through and the cheese is melted. Serve hot.

• • • • • • • •

MEXICAN MEATLOAF

Quintessential meatloaf is given the Southwestern treatment with ground tortilla in place of bread crumbs and a chipotle-spiked ketchup glaze. **Serves 4 to 6**

1 tablespoon vegetable oil

1 medium onion, diced

2 medium carrots, peeled and diced

5 small (6-inch) corn tortillas

1½ pounds ground turkey

½ cup ketchup, divided

1 large egg

1 teaspoon ground cumin

½ teaspoon kosher salt

½ teaspoon chipotle powder

1. Preheat the oven to 400°F. In a large skillet, heat the vegetable oil over medium heat. Add the onions and the carrots and cook, stirring occasionally, until the carrots are tender, 7 to 9 minutes. Let cool slightly.

2. Tear the tortillas into pieces and place in the bowl of a food processor. Pulse until the tortillas resemble coarse crumbs. Transfer to a large bowl and add the turkey, the sautéed onions and carrots, ¼ cup of the ketchup, and the egg, cumin, and salt. Form the mixture into a loaf-shaped mound in the middle of a 9 x 13-inch glass or metal pan. In a small bowl, mix the remaining ¼ cup ketchup with the chipotle powder. Brush the ketchup mixture onto the top and sides of the meatloaf. Bake for about 50 minutes or until the internal temperature registers 160°F when checked with a meat thermometer. Cut into slices and serve hot.

• • • • • • • •

BROCCOLI-CHICKEN CASSEROLE

This creamy, layered dish has a retro appeal—it reminds me of something a 1950s housewife might have served at a dinner party. If you prefer, you could use frozen peas instead of broccoli. Poach some chicken breasts for this recipe, use leftover chicken or turkey meat, or buy a rotisserie chicken. **Serves 8**

2 tablespoons unsalted butter

2 tablespoons all-purpose flour

1½ cups whole milk

2 cups shredded Monterey Jack cheese, divided (8 ounces)

½ teaspoon kosher salt

⅛ teaspoon black pepper

⅛ teaspoon ground nutmeg

6 small (6-inch) corn tortillas

1 pound cooked boneless skinless chicken breast, cut into chunks

1 (16-ounce) bag frozen chopped broccoli, thawed

1. Preheat the oven to 375°F. Spray an 11 x 7-inch baking dish with cooking spray or brush lightly with vegetable oil. In a medium saucepan, melt the butter over medium heat. When it foams, whisk in the flour until it forms a paste. Cook, stirring, for 1 minute, to allow the flour to brown slightly. Gradually whisk in the milk, about ¼ cup at a time, whisking in between additions until smooth. Bring to a simmer over medium heat, then reduce the heat to medium-low and cook until the mixture has thickened, about 5 minutes. Stir in 1 cup of the cheese and cook, stirring, until the cheese has melted and the mixture is smooth. Stir in the salt, pepper, and nutmeg.

2. Line the bottom of the prepared casserole dish with the tortillas, tearing the tortillas to fit the bottom of the pan in a single layer with little overlap. Sprinkle half of the chicken and half of the broccoli over the tortillas. Spoon half of the sauce over the chicken and broccoli, and sprinkle with about ½ cup of the remaining cheese. Repeat with another layer of tortilla, chicken, and broccoli. Spoon the remaining sauce over the dish and sprinkle with the remaining ½ cup cheese. Bake until the casserole is bubbling and the cheese has melted, about 30 minutes. Serve hot.

* * * * * * * * *

FUN WITH TORTILLAS

Mild-tasting, easy to hold, and fun to load up with yummy ingredients, tortillas seem tailor-made creative, fun snacks for kids and adults alike. Whether you roll them around appealing ingredients, bake them for a healthier alternative to store-bought tortilla chips, or use them as a base for fun concoctions, there's no doubt that gourmets of all ages will love preparing and eating these recipes.

PB&J QUESADILLA

Who needs bread? This simple sandwich is made between two tortillas—no more squished sammies! To make it a little healthier, seek out small whole wheat tortillas. If you're packing it for a lunch, don't cook it. **Serves 1**

2 small (6-inch) flour or whole wheat tortillas

1 tablespoon crunchy peanut butter

1 tablespoon jam

1. Spread the peanut butter on one tortilla. Spread the jam on the other tortilla. Press the two pieces together to make a sandwich.

2. Heat a small skillet over medium heat. Place the quesadilla in the pan and cook until the tortilla begins to get toasty and the filling is warmed, about 2 minutes on each side. Remove from the pan and use a knife or a pizza wheel to slice into wedges.

• • • • • • • •

LUNCHBOX TURKEY ROLL-UP

These wraps make a nice change from boring sandwiches. Use your favorite lunchmeat and cheese combination, and if you don't like mustard, try spreading the tortilla with a little mayo or cream cheese. To pack, roll this tightly in plastic wrap or aluminum foil, and be sure to include an ice pack so it stays at a safe, cool temperature until it's eaten. **Serves 1**

1 medium (8-inch) flour tortilla
1 tablespoon yellow mustard
3 slices deli turkey

2 slices American or Colby cheese
¼ cup sprouts
2 dill pickle spears

1. Place the tortilla on a work surface and spread the mustard in a thin, even layer. Arrange the turkey on the tortilla, and place the cheese in the center of the tortilla so that there is cheese the entire length of the tortilla, from top to bottom. Spread the sprouts over the entire tortilla. Place the pickles in a row from top to bottom to one side of the cheese and begin rolling it around the pickles. Continue rolling the tortilla until you have a rolled log shape. If desired, slice the roll in half on the diagonal. If packing in a lunchbox, be sure to include an ice pack so it stays at a safe, cool temperature until it's eaten.

●　●　●　●　●　●　●　●　●

PIZZA-DILLA

These little folded pizzas make a great quick lunch or an after-school snack. It's easy to keep a jar of pasta sauce and a hunk of mozzarella cheese at the ready to make these any time. If you're making them for kids, they'll love to help spread the sauce or sprinkle on the toppings.

Serves 2

2 medium (8-inch) flour tortillas

½ cup prepared tomato sauce (such as pizza sauce or pasta sauce)

1 (4-ounce) can black olives, drained

½ cup shredded mozzarella cheese (2 ounces)

1. Spread a few spoonfuls of tomato sauce on one half of each tortilla, leaving a small border along the edges. Sprinkle black olives and mozzarella cheese over the sauce. Fold the tortilla in half over the sauce, lightly pressing to close.

2. Heat a medium skillet over medium heat. Add one tortilla and cook until the underside is lightly toasted, 2 to 3 minutes. Flip over and cook until the cheese is melted and the second side of the tortilla is lightly toasted, 2 to 3 minutes longer. Let cool for a minute or two, then cut into wedges. Serve hot or warm.

• • • • • • • • •

BAKED TORTILLA CHIPS WITH YOGURT-AVOCADO DIP

This avocado dip is just the right combination of tangy and creamy. Pack it in a small container for a go-to meal or snack, or serve it at a party. **Serves 4 to 6**

Dip:

1 medium ripe avocado

¼ cup plain low-fat yogurt

2 tablespoons freshly squeezed lime juice

¼ teaspoon kosher salt

⅛ teaspoon garlic powder

⅛ teaspoon black pepper

Chips:

4 small (6-inch) flour tortillas

1 tablespoon extra-virgin olive oil

kosher salt

1. To make the dip: Cut the avocado in half, remove the pit, and scoop the flesh into a small bowl. Add the yogurt, lime juice, salt, garlic powder, and pepper. Stir to combine, then puree with an immersion blender until smooth. Cover with plastic wrap pressed against the surface and refrigerate until ready to serve, up 3 hours.

2. To make the chips: Preheat the oven to 375°F. Brush the tortillas with olive oil on both sides. Cut each tortilla into 8 wedges and arrange on a rimmed baking sheet. Sprinkle with salt. Bake until the wedges begin to get crispy, then turn the chips over and bake until crisp and lightly browned, 8 to 10 minutes longer. Let cool completely before serving. Serve the cold dip with the chips.

• • • • • • • •

TORTILLA "FACES"

These fun "faces" are great to make with friends. Gather a group and get creative making each other's faces on tortillas, then dig in (eat the face you made or eat your own face—either way, try not to think about it too hard). Plus, set this fun presentation in front of any preschooler and you'll instantly become the coolest parent ever! It's amazing how much more eagerly veggies will be gobbled up if carrots are hair, broccoli is a beard, and red pepper slices are mouths. **Makes 2 open-faced sandwiches**

1 ounce cream cheese	½ cup shredded Colby cheese (2 ounces)
½ teaspoon ketchup, plus more as needed	2 thin slices red bell pepper
2 small (6-inch) flour tortillas	2 baby carrots
4 black olives	¼ cup raisins

1. In a small bowl, combine the cream cheese and ketchup, stirring until the mixture is smooth and spreadable. Add more ketchup as needed to make a pinker color.

2. Spread the cream cheese mixture on the tortillas. Make the face by using black olives for eyes, shredded cheese for hair, red pepper to make a smile or a frown, and a baby carrot to make a nose. Raisins can be used to make a beard, a mustache, or eyebrows. To eat, kids can fold the whole tortilla in half, or you can cut it into sections with a knife or a pizza wheel.

• • • • • • • • •

PIGS IN A PONCHO WITH SOUTHWESTERN KETCHUP DIP

A riff on pigs in a blanket, this is a fun party food or lunch. And while you might not always have hot dog buns on hand, chances are you have a few flour tortillas around! **Serves 2**

2 slices Colby cheese

2 medium (8-inch) flour tortillas

2 teaspoons yellow mustard

2 hot dogs

¼ cup ketchup

1 tablespoon prepared salsa

¼ teaspoon ground cumin

1. Preheat the oven to 400°F. Place 1 slice of cheese in the middle of a tortilla. Drizzle mustard over the cheese and place a hot dog vertically in the center of the tortilla, with the end almost to the top. Fold the bottom of the tortilla over the hot dog and roll the sides of the tortilla snugly around the hot dog to overlap. Secure with a toothpick and place on a rimmed baking sheet.

2. Bake until the tortilla holds its shape on its own, feels crisp to the touch, and the cheese has melted, 10 to 15 minutes. While the dogs are cooking, mix together the ketchup, salsa, and cumin. Let the hot dogs cool for a few minutes before serving. Serve warm or hot with the Southwestern ketchup dip.

● ● ● ● ● ● ● ●

FISH STICK TACOS WITH SALSA CREAM

It was my husband who hit upon this genius use for frozen fish sticks when he was rooting through the fridge and freezer for something to make for lunch. If you like fish tacos, you'll love this shortcut recipe. It makes a quick family dinner or a fun weekend lunch. **Serves 4**

12 frozen fish sticks

¼ cup prepared salsa

¼ cup sour cream

4 small (6-inch) flour tortillas

1 cup shredded lettuce

1. Cook the fish sticks in the oven according to the package instructions.

2. In a small bowl, combine the salsa and the sour cream. To assemble the tacos, warm the tortillas in the microwave or over an open burner, then fill each tortilla with 3 fish sticks, a handful of shredded lettuce, and a drizzle of the salsa cream. Serve immediately.

• • • • • • • •

TUNA MELT TORTILLAS

The classic tuna melt is reimagined on a tortilla. Serve it open-faced, then roll the sides around it to eat. I sometimes like to use canned salmon in place of tuna, and of course, you can use whatever kind of sliced cheese you have on hand. Swiss and Muenster are particularly tasty alternatives. **Serves 2**

1 (5-ounce) can chunk tuna, drained

1 dill pickle, minced, or 2 tablespoons pickle relish

2 tablespoons minced red bell pepper

1 teaspoon yellow mustard

2 tablespoons light mayonnaise

2 small (6-inch) flour tortillas

2 slices American cheese

kosher salt and black pepper

1. Preheat the oven's broiler. In a bowl, combine the tuna, pickle, and bell pepper. In a small bowl, stir together the mustard and mayonnaise. Stir the mustard-mayonnaise mixture into the tuna mixture. Season to taste with salt and pepper.

2. Place the tortillas on a rimmed baking sheet and place under the broiler until warmed through and beginning to brown, about 1 minute. Turn the tortillas over and cook for 1 minute on the second side. Divide the tuna mixture between the tortillas, mounding in the center, leaving about ½-inch along the edge of the tortilla. Place cheese slices over the tuna and return the baking sheet to the broiler. Broil until the cheese melts and begins to bubble, 1 to 2 minutes, watching carefully to make sure it doesn't burn. Transfer the tuna melts to two plates and serve immediately. Tortillas can be eaten open-face, with a knife and fork, or can be folded or rolled to eat by hand.

· · · · · · · ·

MAKE YOUR OWN TACO BAR

For a party, a do-it-yourself taco bar is an easy, inexpensive, no-fuss way to feed a crowd, and it has universal appeal—who doesn't like tacos, especially when you can make them yourself? If you also warm up two 15-ounce cans of refried beans and offer flour tortillas, you can give guests the option of making their own burritos as well as tacos. If you don't have taco seasoning on hand, simply mix 2 teaspoons ground cumin with 1 teaspoon salt and ¼ teaspoon garlic powder. **Serves 8 to 10**

1 tablespoon vegetable oil

1 pound ground beef or turkey

1 tablespoon taco seasoning

2 cups shredded Colby cheese (8 ounces)

1 (4-ounce) can sliced black olives, drained

1 cup low-fat sour cream or plain Greek-style yogurt

1 large head iceberg lettuce, shredded

2 medium avocados, pitted, peeled, diced, and squirted with juice of ½ lime to keep from browning

2 large globe tomatoes, diced

1 (12-ounce) jar prepared mild salsa

10 small (6-inch) soft corn or flour tortillas

1. Heat the vegetable oil in a large skillet over medium-high heat. Add the ground beef or turkey and cook, breaking up the pieces into small chunks, until browned and cooked through, about 10 minutes. Sprinkle with taco seasoning and stir to coat the meat completely. Lift the meat out with a slotted spoon to drain away excess fat, and transfer to a bowl. Cover with aluminum foil to keep warm, or transfer to a slow cooker set to "keep warm."

2. Place all of the toppings in bowls with serving spoons, including the cheese, black olives, yogurt, lettuce, avocados, tomatoes, and salsa. Arrange the meat and toppings on a counter or a table, buffet-style.

3. Heat the tortillas spread on a baking pan in a preheated 300°F oven, or over an open burner for about 10 seconds on each side, or stacked in the microwave on high power for about 20 seconds. Place the warm tortillas in a tortilla warmer or wrap them loosely in a clean dishtowel.

4. Invite each guest to assemble their own tacos with the tortillas, meat, and toppings.

· · · · · · · · ·

CINNAMON TORTILLA CRISPS WITH YOGURT DIP

When a sweet craving strikes, this sweet and tangy yogurt dip makes a healthier option. The tortilla crisps will keep for a few days in an airtight container or zip-top bag. Use whole wheat tortillas to make this snack even healthier. If you're making this recipe for a party or for kids, try cutting the tortilla crisps into different simple shapes with cookie cutters. **Serves 4 to 6**

Cinnamon Tortilla Crisps:

4 large (10 to 12-inch) flour tortillas

1 tablespoon unsalted butter, melted

1 teaspoon ground cinnamon

2 teaspoons sugar

Yogurt Dip:

½ cup light cream cheese, softened (4 ounces)

½ cup low-fat vanilla yogurt

2 teaspoons honey

1. To make the crisps: Preheat the oven to 375°F. Brush the tortillas on both sides with the melted butter. In a small bowl, combine the cinnamon and sugar. Cut the tortillas into wedges or squares (or use cookie cutters to cut them into shapes). Spread them in a single layer on a baking sheet. Prick the tortillas all over with a fork and sprinkle them with half the cinnamon-sugar mixture. Bake for 10 minutes, turn over the crisps, sprinkle the other side with cinnamon-sugar, and bake until crisp but not brown, 7 to 10 minutes longer. Remove from the oven and let cool completely on the baking sheet.

2. To make the yogurt dip: Combine the cream cheese, yogurt and honey in a medium bowl. Use an immersion blender or a hand mixer to blend until smooth. Transfer to a serving dish and serve with the cinnamon tortilla crisps.

• • • • • • • • •

ICE CREAM SUNDAES IN COCOA TORTILLA BOWLS

A chocolate-dusted tortilla bowl makes a cute presentation for ice cream sundaes. Use any flavor ice cream you like. **Serves 4**

4 small (6-inch) flour tortillas

1 tablespoon melted unsalted butter

1 (1-ounce) packet prepared hot cocoa mix

1 pint ice cream

½ cup chocolate syrup

canned or homemade whipped cream, to serve

4 maraschino cherries

1. Preheat the oven to 375°F. Prick the tortillas all over with a fork. Brush both sides of the tortillas with the melted butter and sprinkle with the hot cocoa mix on both sides. Fit the tortillas into small ovenproof bowls or ramekins, about 5 inches in diameter, crimping the sides of the tortillas loosely to fit them into the bowls. Bake until the tortillas hold their shape on their own, about 10 minutes. Remove them from the bowls and finish baking them on a sheet pan or directly on the oven rack until the tortillas are crisp and just beginning to brown, 5 to 10 minutes longer. Let cool completely.

2. Place a scoop of ice cream in each tortilla bowl. Top with a drizzle of chocolate syrup, a dollop of whipped cream, and a maraschino cherry. Serve immediately.

• • • • • • • •

SWEET ENDINGS

The neutral flavor of corn and flour tortillas lend themselves nicely to desserts. And using them in no-bake treats or as a stand-in for pastry dough makes me wonder why they don't get the sweet treatment more often! Try using tortillas to make some of these creative desserts and you'll discover how perfectly tortillas work with sweet ingredients like chocolate, fruit, and creamy fillings.

NUTELLA® QUESADILLAS

Toast up some tortillas stuffed with a sweet filling and you've got dessert in minutes! Kids in particular love the novelty of a sweet quesadilla. It's a great way to use up the last few tortillas in the bag. For a fun variation, make s'mores quesadillas by replacing the jam with marshmallow fluff. **Serves 4**

4 small (6-inch) flour tortillas

¼ cup Nutella (chocolate-hazelnut spread)

¼ cup raspberry jam

prepared whipped cream, for garnish (optional)

1. Spread the Nutella on 2 tortillas and the jam on the other 2 tortillas. Sandwich the tortillas together in pairs, with the fillings on the inside. Heat a dry skillet over medium heat. Working one at a time, toast the quesadillas until the tortillas are light brown and the filling is a little melty, 1 to 2 minutes on each side. Let cool for a few moments before cutting into wedges with a knife or a pizza wheel. If desired, garnish each wedge with a small dollop of whipped cream.

· · · · · · · ·

PINEAPPLE CHEESECAKE WITH TORTILLA CRUST

The creamy, sweet filling and the mellow pineapple flavor of this cheesecake are the perfect foil for a crust made of corn tortillas.

Serves 8 to 10

10 small (6-inch) corn tortillas

¼ cup plus 2 tablespoons brown sugar, divided

2 tablespoons melted unsalted butter

¼ cup warm water

3 (8-ounce) packages cream cheese

½ cup granulated sugar

1 (20-ounce) can crushed pineapple in juice, drained, juice reserved

3 large eggs

1 teaspoon vanilla extract

1. Preheat the oven to 400°F. Tear the tortillas into pieces and place in the bowl of a food processor with ¼ cup of the brown sugar. Process until the mixture resembles fine bread crumbs. With the motor running, drizzle in the butter and warm water until the mixture forms a clumpy dough. Turn out into a 9-inch springform baking pan and press the crust evenly into the bottom of the pan, pressing it about 1 inch up the sides. Bake until the crust is golden on the edges and dry to the touch, about 15 minutes.

2. While the crust is baking, make the filling: Place the cream cheese and granulated sugar in a bowl and use a handheld mixer or a stand mixer on medium speed to beat the mixture until smooth. Add the pineapple juice and mix on low speed until smooth. Gradually beat in the eggs one at a time, then beat in the vanilla.

3. Pour the filling over the cooked crust and return to the oven. Bake until the filling is set, 45 to 50 minutes.

4. In a medium bowl, mix the crushed pineapple with the remaining 2 tablespoons brown sugar. Spread the pineapple over the cheesecake and bake until the sugar looks syrupy, about 10 minutes longer. Let cool completely before removing from the pan. Slide a butter knife around the perimeter of the pan to loosen it before releasing the sides and removing the cheesecake.

· · · · · · · · ·

TORTILLA-LIME BARK

You know the preponderance of crazy candy bars with ingredients like bacon, wasabi, curry, and various fancy salts? I saw one once that contained tortilla chips, lime, and chile powder—it was so unusual I just had to buy it. To my surprise, the weird combination totally worked! The tangy lime offset the rich chocolate flavor, and the tortilla chips added a nice crunch and saltiness. I was inspired to dream up this chocolate bark recipe, which makes a good hostess gift or thank-you token for a teacher, your dog walker, or any chocolate lover in your life. Tempering the chocolate helps it achieve a shiny appearance and gives it a nice snap when it's bitten or broken. **Makes about 32 small pieces**

1 (16-ounce) package semisweet chocolate chips

1 cup salted tortilla chips, crushed into small pieces (about 1 ounce)

2 teaspoons grated lime zest

¼ teaspoon red chile powder or ground cayenne pepper

1. Line a rimmed baking sheet or a 9 x 13-inch metal baking pan with parchment paper and place it in the freezer.

2. Temper the chocolate: Place the chocolate chips in a double boiler or in a heatproof bowl set over a saucepan of simmering water (the water should not touch the bottom of the bowl). Gradually melt the chocolate, stirring frequently with a rubber spatula, until smooth and completely melted. Keep heating the chocolate until it reaches a temperature of 110 to 115°F when checked with a candy thermometer or an instant-read thermometer. Remove the chocolate from the heat and cool, stirring and scraping the chocolate from the sides and bottom of the bowl to incorporate air, until the temperature drops below 84°F. Return the chocolate to the double boiler and heat briefly, stirring, until the chocolate reaches 89°F.

3. Remove the prepared baking pan from the freezer and spread the chocolate over the parchment paper in an even layer about ¼ inch thick. Sprinkle the tortilla chips and lime zest evenly over the melted chocolate. Lightly dust with the chile powder or cayenne pepper. Return the pan to the freezer and freeze until set, about 1 hour. Use a knife or a pizza wheel to cut the bark into small pieces. Keep cool.

• • • • • • • •

MEXICAN CHOCOLATE PUDDING IN TORTILLA CUPS

Did you know that you can make chocolate pudding simply by thickening hot cocoa with a bit of cornstarch? This pudding recipe is super easy, and it's such a cute presentation when served in little crispy tortilla cups. Look for Abuelita brand hot cocoa mix in the hot beverages aisle or the international foods section of your supermarket. If you can't find it, use any hot cocoa mix and add ½ teaspoon of cinnamon. **Serves 6**

2 teaspoons sugar

1 teaspoon ground cinnamon, plus more for garnish

6 small (6-inch) flour tortillas

1 tablespoon melted unsalted butter

3 cups whole milk, divided

¼ cup cornstarch

4 (1-ounce) packets hot cocoa mix, preferably Abuelita brand

1 ounce semisweet chocolate, chopped

1 teaspoon vanilla extract

prepared whipped cream, for garnish

1. Preheat the oven to 375°F. In a small bowl, stir together the sugar and 1 teaspoon ground cinnamon. Warm the tortillas in the microwave for 20 seconds. Brush them with the melted butter on both sides, sprinkle with the cinnamon and sugar, and prick the tortillas all over with a fork. Fit the tortillas into muffin tins, gathering the sides gently to fit them into the cups. Bake for 15 minutes or until crisp. Let cool.

2. Heat 2½ cups of the milk in a medium saucepan over medium heat until steaming. In a small bowl, combine the cornstarch with the remaining ½ cup milk, whisking until smooth. When the milk in the pan steams, stir in the hot cocoa mix, whisking until fully blended. Whisk in the cornstarch mixture and cook, stirring frequently, until the mixture comes to a boil, about 5 minutes. Stir in the chocolate until it melts, then reduce the heat to low and simmer, stirring occasionally, until the pudding has thickened, about 5 minutes longer. Remove from the heat and stir in the vanilla extract. Transfer the pudding to a bowl and let cool until warm. Cover with plastic wrap, pressing it against the surface of the pudding to prevent a skin from forming. Refrigerate until cool. To serve, spoon the pudding into the tortilla cups. Garnish with a dollop of whipped cream and a sprinkle of cinnamon.

• • • • • • • •

CREAM-FILLED CARDAMOM TORTILLA BITES

These elegant little one-bite treats are just the thing to serve at an afternoon tea or on the dessert tray at a cocktail party. Cardamom is a Middle Eastern spice often used in Scandinavian and East Indian cooking; it has a spicy-sweet flavor. This recipe for pastry cream is adapted from the very useful baking website Joy of Baking (www.joyofbaking.com). **Makes 2 dozen bites**

1 teaspoon ground cardamom

⅓ cup plus 2 teaspoons sugar, divided

4 medium (8-inch) flour tortillas

2 tablespoons melted unsalted butter

3 large egg yolks

⅓ cup all-purpose flour

pinch kosher salt

1¼ cups whole milk

1 teaspoon vanilla extract

2 teaspoons Kahlúa or 1 tablespoon strong black coffee

1. Preheat the oven to 350°F. In a small bowl, stir together the cardamom and 2 teaspoons of the sugar. Brush the tortillas with melted butter on both sides. Using a 2-inch metal biscuit cutter, cut out about 12 rounds from each tortilla. Place on a baking sheet. Prick all over with a fork and sprinkle with the cardamom-sugar mixture. Bake until crispy, 10 to 12 minutes. Let cool on the baking sheet.

2. In a medium bowl, whisk together the egg yolks and the remaining ⅓ cup sugar. Whisk in the flour and the salt. Heat the milk in a medium saucepan over medium-low heat until steaming. Whisk a few spoonfuls of the milk at a time into the egg mixture, gradually warming the eggs without scrambling them. As the mixture heats up, add more milk to the eggs until it's all mixed in. Pour the milk and egg mixture back into the saucepan and cook over medium heat. Stir constantly until the mixture thickens and begins to bubble. Continue to cook for 1 to 2 minutes longer, then remove from the heat and stir in the vanilla extract and the Kahlúa or black coffee. Let cool completely.

3. Turn over half of the tortilla crisps so the cardamom is facing down (the cardamom coating should be on the outside of both sides of the assembled "sandwich"). Transfer the cooled pastry cream into a large zip-top bag. Cut the corner off the bag and pipe onto half of the tortilla crisps, turned over so the cardamom coating is on the underside. Top with the remaining tortilla crisps cardamom-side up. Serve within a few hours of making, as the tortillas will begin to get soggy.

· · · · · · · · ·

APPLE-CINNAMON TORTILLA POCKETS

In Georgia, where I live, fried pies are available at just about every festival and side-of-the-road farm stand. They're typically filled with peaches or apples, our state's two main fruit crops. I decided to use tortillas to make a slightly healthier baked version. Firm, tart green apples, like Granny Smith, are my favorite for this recipe, but you can use any good baking apple. **Serves 6**

4 small apples, cored, peeled, and thinly sliced

2 tablespoons freshly squeezed lemon juice

1 tablespoon cornstarch

2 tablespoons sugar

½ teaspoon ground cinnamon

6 medium (8-inch) flour tortillas

1 cup confectioners' sugar

½ teaspoon vanilla extract

2 tablespoons whole milk, or more as needed

1. Preheat the oven to 375°F. Place the apples in a medium bowl. Add the lemon juice, cornstarch, sugar, and cinnamon, and toss to combine.

2. Fill a small dish with water. Spoon the apple filling onto one half of each tortilla. Dip your finger in the water and moisten about a 1-inch border of the tortilla. Fold the tortilla over the filling and press down very firmly to seal. With a sharp knife, cut a slit or two in the top of each pie to allow steam to escape. Bake until the tortillas are crisp and lightly browned, about 25 minutes.

3. In a small bowl, combine the confectioners' sugar and vanilla extract. Stir in just enough milk to create a very thick but pourable icing. Drizzle the icing over the pies while still warm. Let the icing set before serving warm or at room temperature.

• • • • • • • • •

ICE CREAM TACO TREATS

When I started brainstorming dessert ideas for this book, my husband begged me to include his favorite ice cream novelty: Choco Tacos. These treats do indeed resemble a taco, with a "tortilla" shell made of wafer cookie, ice cream filling, and a chocolate and peanut coating. I discovered that the inherent sweetness of corn tortillas is accentuated if it's combined with sweet ingredients like chocolate and ice cream. Make these for a kids' get-together. You'll find Magic Shell topping at the supermarket with the other ice cream toppings. **4 servings**

4 small (6-inch) corn tortillas

1 pint vanilla ice cream with chocolate ribbon

8 ounces Magic Shell ice cream topping

¼ cup crushed peanuts

1. Preheat the oven to 350°F. Stack the tortillas and microwave on high power for 20 seconds. Drape the tortillas over the sides of two loaf pans and bake to form the tortillas into taco shells. Bake until the tortillas are crisp but still have a little give when the shells are pulled open slightly, about 15 minutes. Allow to cool.

2. Remove the ice cream from the freezer for 10 minutes to soften. Using a small spatula, stuff the ice cream into the taco shells, filling the shell completely and smoothing the ice cream along the edge of the tortilla. Holding over a bowl or a plate, drizzle the Magic Shell over the exposed ice cream and edge of the tortilla, then quickly sprinkle with the peanuts before the Magic Shell dries. Place the ice cream tacos on a baking sheet or a freezer-safe plate and freeze until very firm, for at least several hours.

* * * * * * * * *

MEXICAN CANNOLI

I've always liked the creamy ricotta filling of cannoli, but I find the shells greasy and heavy. Since flour tortillas, when baked, have such a crispy, light texture, I decided to try subbing them for the cannoli pastry in this traditional Italian dessert. If I had an Italian nonna, I'm sure she'd be none too happy to learn that it actually works quite well! Luckily I don't, but I think my Mexican grandma would probably like this recipe, especially if I made it with her homemade tortillas. **Makes 8 cannoli**

1 pound ricotta cheese, drained for 30 minutes

4 small (6-inch) flour tortillas

¾ cup confectioners' sugar

½ teaspoon vanilla extract

½ teaspoon almond extract

¼ teaspoon ground cinnamon

½ cup mini chocolate chips

1. Place the ricotta cheese in cheesecloth and suspend it over a bowl. Let drain for 30 minutes to 1 hour to remove excess water.

2. Preheat the oven to 350°F. Stack the tortillas and microwave at high power until pliable, about 15 seconds. Roll the tortillas into 1-inch wide tubes, securing with toothpicks if necessary. Place on a baking sheet seam-side down and bake for 15 minutes or until crisp. Remove the toothpicks and cool completely on the baking sheet.

3. In a medium bowl, stir together the strained ricotta, confectioners' sugar, vanilla extract, almond extract, and cinnamon. Spoon into a large zip-top bag, seal the bag, and cut a small hole in the corner. Pipe the filling into the tortilla rolls from both ends to fill the rolls completely. Put the chocolate chips in a small, shallow dish and dip the ends of the cannoli into the chips so that they coat the ricotta filling. Place the cannoli on a tray, wrap loosely with plastic wrap, and chill for at least 1 hour, or up to 6 hours. These are best eaten on the same day they're prepared, as the tortillas will eventually get soggy.

• • • • • • • •

CARAMELIZED BANANA AND PEANUT TOSTADAS

Sweet and indulgent, this treat is a fun dessert to serve for a romantic dinner for two. Just be sure to allow time after your meal to prepare it, as it's best made just before it's eaten. If you don't want to use rum in the sauce, you can substitute an equal amount of orange juice.

Serves 2

vegetable oil, for frying

2 small (6-inch) corn tortillas

2 small bananas

2 tablespoons unsalted butter

¼ cup brown sugar

2 tablespoons dark rum

½ cup roasted, salted peanuts, coarsely chopped

prepared whipped cream, for garnish

1. Heat about ½ inch of vegetable oil in a medium skillet over high heat until shimmering. Line a plate with paper towels. When the oil is hot, add 1 tortilla and fry until crisp, about 30 seconds on each side. Transfer the tortilla to the paper towel–lined plate. Repeat with the remaining tortilla.

2. Cut the bananas in half crosswise, then split them in half again lengthwise. Dispose of the oil in the skillet, wipe out the skillet with a paper towel, place it over medium heat, and add the butter. When the butter melts, add the brown sugar and cook, stirring, until dissolved, about 2 minutes. Add the bananas, cut-side down. Cook for 1 minute undisturbed, then turn over with tongs and cook 1 minute longer. Drizzle the rum into the pan and cook for 30 seconds, using a spoon or the tongs to stir the rum into the brown sugar mixture around the bananas. Place the fried tortillas on two plates. Arrange 4 banana pieces on each tostada and drizzle the sauce on top. Garnish with peanuts and a dollop of whipped cream.

• • • • • • • •

CHURRO-STYLE TORTILLAS WITH MEXICAN CHOCOLATE DIPPING SAUCE

Our friends Stephen and Ursula loved a little Latin restaurant in the Brooklyn neighborhood where we all once lived. In particular, they were in love with a dessert of churros—Mexican fried dough that's a common street fair food—with an unctuous Mexican chocolate sauce for dipping. I have a weakness for churros too, and I was pleased to discover that if you fry strips of flour tortillas in a little butter, and dust them with cinnamon-sugar, you can replicate this fiesta favorite. If I'm serving this to grown-ups only, I like to stir in a little cayenne or chile powder for an unexpected kick. **Serves 4**

6 ounces semisweet chocolate chips

½ cup heavy cream

1 tablespoon light corn syrup

2½ teaspoons ground cinnamon, divided

½ teaspoon vanilla extract

⅛ teaspoon cayenne pepper or chile pepper (optional)

1 tablespoon sugar

2 tablespoons unsalted butter, plus more as needed

4 small (6-inch) flour tortillas, cut into 1-inch strips, plus more as needed

1. Place the chocolate chips in a medium bowl. In a small saucepan over medium heat, combine the cream and corn syrup and heat just until it comes to a simmer. Pour the cream mixture over the chocolate chips and stir with a spatula until the chips are melted and the sauce is smooth and shiny. Stir in ½ teaspoon of the cinnamon, the vanilla extract, and the cayenne pepper, if using. Cover with aluminum foil to keep warm.

2. In a small bowl, combine the remaining 2 teaspoons cinnamon and the sugar. Melt the butter over medium heat in a large saucepan. Add the tortilla strips in a single layer, working in batches if needed to avoid overcrowding. Fry the tortillas undisturbed until the undersides are golden and puffy, $1\frac{1}{2}$ to 2 minutes. Turn over and fry until evenly browned, 1 to 2 minutes longer. Add more butter to the pan if needed and fry the remaining tortillas. Transfer to a plate and sprinkle both sides with the cinnamon-sugar mixture.

3. Pour the chocolate sauce into individual small bowls or demitasse cups, if desired, and serve with the warm tortilla strips for dipping. The sauce can be made ahead of time and stored for up to several days, covered and refrigerated. Reheat it in a heatproof bowl set over simmering water.

· · · · · · · · ·

APPENDIX

Making Your Own Tortillas

While the recipes in this book call for store-bought tortillas, making your own tortillas from scratch is fun, easy, and requires little in the way of ingredients and special equipment. I've experimented with electric and manual tortilla presses, and in the end, I found that a little wooden rolling pin and a flour-dusted cutting board is best for forming the tortillas, while a dry skillet (I use my cast-iron crêpe pan) is ideal for cooking them.

These homemade tortillas can be used in a number of the recipes within the book, particularly for tacos, cut up and baked for chips, or torn into pieces to go into casseroles.

FLOUR TORTILLAS

Homemade flour tortillas are soft, thick, and fresh-tasting. They're worth making every so often for a nice treat. I like eating them hot out of the pan, folded over a slice of queso fresco, or slathered with butter and sprinkled with cinnamon-sugar. Homemade flour tortillas also make fantastic baked tortilla chips. **Makes 12 small (6-inch) or 8 medium (8-inch) tortillas**

2 cups all-purpose flour	¼ cup vegetable shortening
½ teaspoon fine kosher or sea salt	½ cup warm water
¼ teaspoon baking powder	

1. In a medium bowl, combine the flour, salt, and baking powder, stirring with a fork to combine. Work the shortening into the dry ingredients, using a pastry knife or your clean fingers to rub the shortening into the flour mixture until it resembles crumbs. While stirring with the fork, drizzle the water into the mixture, adding enough to make a clumpy dough. Turn the dough out on a lightly floured work surface and knead for 30 seconds or so, just until the mixture forms a smooth dough that is moist but not too sticky. Add more flour or water as needed. Let the dough rest for 10 minutes, covered with a cloth, to allow the glutens to relax and the flour to absorb the liquid.

2. Using a knife, a pastry bench scraper, or your hands, divide the dough into 12 equal pieces for small tortillas or 8 pieces for medium tortillas. Roll each piece of dough into a smooth ball. Cover the balls with the cloth and let rest for another 10 minutes so the glutens will relax again and the tortillas will be easier to roll out.

3. Heat a griddle or a dry skillet over medium-high heat. On a lightly floured work surface, use a rolling pin to roll out a piece of dough into a thin round, no more than ⅛ inch thick. Place the tortilla in the skillet and cook for about 30 seconds, or until dry and lightly browned on the underside. Turn over and cook for 30 seconds longer. Transfer to a plate and keep warm under a clean dishtowel. Repeat the rolling and cooking process with the remaining tortillas, stacking the cooked tortillas on the cloth-covered plate to keep warm.

Note: To use an electric tortilla press, follow the instructions in Steps 1 and 2. Heat the tortilla press and lightly spray or brush with vegetable oil. Flatten one of the dough balls and place it in the center of the press. Close the press gently with a few pulses, pressing the dough flat. Cook for 10 seconds, until dry and lightly browned, and remove.

CORN TORTILLAS

With only three ingredients, corn tortillas are super-easy to make once you master the technique. And while they're thicker and more fragile than commercially available corn tortillas (and, unless you're an expert, not as perfectly round), their fresh flavor is fantastic. The dough is easy to mix up; the trick is rolling the tortillas thin enough, and working them into an approximate circular shape. Once you get good enough, you can roll the next tortilla out as the previous one cooks, cutting down on the time it takes to make them. Masa harina, the flour traditionally used to make corn tortillas, is also often called corn masa flour. **Makes 8 small (5 to 6-inch) tortillas**

1 cup masa harina

generous pinch kosher salt

¾ cup room-temperature water, or as needed

1. In a medium bowl, combine the masa harina and the salt with a fork. Gradually stir in the water until the mixture forms a clumpy dough. Turn the dough out on a work surface and pat or knead the dough into a smooth ball. Divide into 8 equal pieces, about 1 inch in diameter, and roll each into a ball. Cover with a damp paper towel.

2. Place one dough ball on a sheet of parchment paper. Press it flat, then place another sheet of parchment paper on top and use a rolling pin to roll it out into a circle, by turning the rolling pin in different angles as you roll. Roll the dough out into the thinnest circle you can make.

3. Heat a dry skillet or griddle over high heat. Carefully pull the top piece of parchment off the tortilla. Pick up the parchment with the tortilla stuck to it, and turn the tortilla onto the flat of your hand. Carefully pull the parchment off to avoid ripping the tortilla. Place the tortilla on the hot skillet or griddle and cook for about 45 seconds, until the underside is dry to the touch, but not yet browned. Turn the tortilla over and cook on the other side for 45 seconds longer. Place the tortilla on a plate and cover

TORTILLAS TO THE RESCUE COOKBOOK

with a clean dishtowel to keep warm, and repeat the rolling and cooking process with the remaining tortillas.

MULTIGRAIN TORTILLAS

For healthier tortillas, you can use whole-grain flours or alternatives to all-purpose flour to make tortillas. In this recipe I've used whole wheat flour and spelt flour to make a nutty, hearty tortilla. Feel free to experiment with combinations of your favorite whole-grain flours.

Makes 8 medium (8-inch) tortillas

1 cup whole wheat flour

1 cup spelt flour

½ teaspoon kosher salt

½ teaspoon baking powder

¼ cup vegetable shortening or oil

½ cup warm water

1. In a medium bowl, combine the whole wheat flour, spelt flour, salt, and baking powder, stirring with a fork to combine. Work the vegetable oil into the dry ingredients, using a pastry knife or your clean fingers to rub the oil into the flour mixture until it resembles crumbs. While stirring with the fork, drizzle the water into the mixture, adding enough to make a clumpy dough. Turn the dough out on a lightly floured work surface and knead for 30 seconds or so, just until the mixture forms a smooth dough that is moist but not too sticky. Add more flour or water as needed. Let the dough rest for 10 minutes, covered with a cloth, to allow the glutens to relax and the flour to absorb the liquid.

2. Using a knife, a pastry bench scraper, or your hands, divide the dough into 8 pieces. Roll each piece of dough into a smooth ball. Cover the balls with the cloth and let rest for another 10 minutes so the glutens will relax again and the tortillas will be easier to roll out.

3. Heat a griddle or a dry skillet over medium-high heat. On a lightly floured work surface, use a rolling pin to roll out a piece of dough into a thin round, no more than ⅛ inch thick. Place the tortilla in the skillet and cook for about 30 seconds, or until dry and lightly browned on the underside. Turn over and cook for 30 seconds longer. Transfer to a plate and keep warm under a clean dishtowel. Repeat the rolling and cooking process with the remaining tortillas, stacking the cooked tortillas on the cloth-covered plate to keep warm.

SWEET FLOUR TORTILLAS

These tortillas have a hint of sweetness, thanks to the inclusion of honey, and a tender texture because butter is used instead of shortening. I love eating them for breakfast, alongside scrambled eggs. They're also delicious spread with jam or a bit of cream cheese or soft goat cheese. **Makes 12 small (6-inch) or 8 medium (8-inch) tortillas**

2 cups all-purpose flour

½ teaspoon fine kosher or sea salt

¼ teaspoon baking powder

2 tablespoons honey

¼ cup melted unsalted butter

½ cup warm water

1. In a medium bowl, combine the flour, salt, and baking powder, stirring with a fork to combine. Stir in the honey and the melted butter. While stirring with the fork, drizzle the water into the mixture, adding enough to make a clumpy dough. Turn the dough out on a lightly floured work surface and knead for 30 seconds or so, just until the mixture forms a smooth dough that is moist but not too sticky. Add more flour or water as needed. Let the dough rest for 10 minutes, covered with a cloth, to allow the glutens to relax and the flour to absorb the liquid.

2. Using a knife, a pastry bench scraper, or your hands, divide the dough into 8 pieces. Roll each piece of dough into a smooth ball. Cover the balls with the cloth and let rest for another 10 minutes so the glutens will relax again and the tortillas will be easier to roll out.

3. Heat a griddle or a dry skillet over medium-high heat. On a lightly floured work surface, use a rolling pin to roll out a piece of dough into a thin round, no more than ⅛ inch thick. Place the tortilla in the skillet and cook for about 30 seconds, or until dry and lightly browned on the underside. Turn over and cook for 30 seconds longer. Transfer to a plate and keep warm under a clean dishtowel. Repeat the rolling and cooking process with the remaining tortillas, stacking the cooked tortillas on the cloth-covered plate to keep warm.

Tortilla Resources

The following are resources for ingredients and kitchenware items that can help you make homemade tortillas, or prepare store-bought tortillas.

Berridge Farms
Fresh and frozen green and red chiles
www.hatchnmgreenchile.com
575-635-4680

Chicago Metallic
Baked-taco racks, tortilla-shell makers
www.chicagometallicbakeware.com
800-238-BAKE

IMUSA
Comals, griddles, manual tortilla presses, tortilla warmers
www.imusausa.com
800-850-2501

La Tortilla Oven
Cloth tortilla warmers
www.latortillaoven.com
626-674-2531

Las Cosas
Tortilla-shell makers, tortilla warmers, tortilla presses, tortilla fry baskets
www.lascosascooking.com
877-229-7184

MexGrocer.com

Tortilla presses, tortilla warmers, skillets, comals, tortillas, masa harina, salsa, spices, chiles

www.mexgrocer.com

877-463-9476

Norpro

Tortilla-bowl makers, manual tortilla presses, tortilla keepers, tortilla fry baskets, taco racks, taco presses

www.norpro.com

425-261-1000

Santa Fe School of Cooking

Tortilla warmers and rolling pins (in-store only), Southwestern spices, blue corn flour, salsa

www.santafeschoolofcooking.com

800-982-4688

Texas Rolling Pins

Tortilla rolling pins, tortilla warmers

www.texasrollingpins.com

Tortilla Press Store

Electric tortilla presses

www.tortillapressstore.com

Conversions

MEASURE	EQUIVALENT	METRIC
1 teaspoon	--	5 milliliters
1 tablespoon	3 teaspoons	14.8 milliliters
1 cup	16 tablespoons	236.8 milliliters
1 pint	2 cups	473.6 milliliters
1 quart	4 cups	947.2 milliliters
1 liter	4 cups + 3½ tablespoons	1000 milliliters
1 ounce (dry)	2 tablespoons	28.35 grams
1 pound	16 ounces	453.49 grams
2.21 pounds	35.3 ounces	1 kilogram
270°F / 350°F	--	132°C / 177°C

RECIPE INDEX

A

Apple-Cinnamon Tortilla Pockets, 182–83

Avocado and Leek Omelet Wrap, 31–32

B

Bacon, Egg, and Cheese Roll, 26

Baked Tortilla Chips with Yogurt-Avocado Dip, 161

Baked Wontons with Sweet-and-Sour Dipping Sauce, 48–49

BBQ and Slaw Wrap, 81–82

Black Bean Soup in Tortilla Bowls, 57–58

BLTA tacos, 83

Broccoli-Cheddar Quiche, 115–16

Broccoli-Chicken Casserole, 155–56

Burger Pouches, 102–103

Burrito Casserole, 151–52

C

Calabacitas Burrito, 74–75

Calexico Burrito, 73

California Burrito, 76–77

Caramelized Banana and Peanut Tostadas, 187–88

Carne Asada Tacos, 108–109

Ceviche Roll-Ups, 84

L

M

N

P

R

S

T

U

W

Y

ABOUT THE AUTHOR

Jessica Harlan has written about food and cooking for nearly twenty years for many print and online publications, including About.com, *Clean Eating*, *Town & Country*, *Mobil Travel Guide*, Gaiam.com, *Pilates Style*, and *Arthritis Today*. A graduate of the Institute of Culinary Education in New York City, she has honed her skills and areas of expertise by developing recipes for major food brands, catering intimate parties, and getting involved in food-related charities. Her first cookbook, *Ramen to the Rescue*, was published by Ulysses Press in 2011, and she co-authored the book *Quinoa Cuisine* with Kelly Sparwasser (Ulysses Press, 2012). She lives in Atlanta, Georgia.